WINNING THE

SPIRITUAL WAR

DON STEWART

TABLE OF CONTENTS

WINNING THE SPIRITUAL WAR

How to Have Victory over the World, the Flesh, and the Devil

The Bible says that each believer inherits three enemies—the world, the flesh, and the devil. In this book, we will concentrate on two of them: the world and the flesh. We will see what they represent and how believers can have victory over them.

Who are the Believer's Enemies?
(The World, the flesh, and the Devil)

Christians are living between two worlds. We are living in our present sinful age, with the promise of a better time in the age to come. While we live in this world we are faced with temptations, suffering, sickness, and death.

Indeed, believers are engaged in spiritual warfare in this present, evil age. In fact, Scripture teaches that we face three foes—the world, the flesh, and the devil.

ENEMY NUMBER 1: THE "WORLD SYSTEM"

The world actually speaks of the present "world system." It is a world system that tries to tear us down. John wrote:

> Do not love this world nor the things it offers you, for when you love the world, you do not have the love of the Father in you. For the world offers only a craving for physical pleasure, a craving for everything we see, and pride in our achievements and possessions. These are not from the Father, but are from this world. And this world is fading away, along with everything that people crave. But anyone who does what pleases God will live forever (1 John 2:15-17 NLT).

This world, in which we live, does not have the same priorities as God the Father. Indeed, this present, evil world system is at odds with the things of God.

When Paul wrote to the Galatians, he described the world system as something which is evil. He put it this way:

> He died for our sins, just as God our Father planned, in order to rescue us from this evil world in which we live (Galatians 1:4 NLT).

The world system is evil in the sense that it refuses to acknowledge God. Instead, it is interested in all things sinful.

The good news is that Jesus Christ allows believers to have victory over this present, evil world system. John wrote the following:

> Loving God means keeping his commandments, and his commandments are not burdensome. For every child of God defeats this evil world, and we achieve this victory through our faith (1 John 5:3,4 NLT).

The believer can overcome the evil world system through Jesus Christ. This is the promise of God's Word.

ENEMY NUMBER 2: THE FLESH (THE OLD SIN NATURE)

Apart from this world system, we have a second enemy, the flesh. The flesh is our old sinful nature. It is the nature we inherit at birth. The Bible says that Adam and Eve had sons and daughters in their own likeness:

> When Adam was 130 years old, his son Seth was born, and Seth was the very image of his father. After the birth of Seth, Adam lived another 800 years, and he had other sons and daughters (Genesis 5:3,4 NLT).

The likeness of Adam was in his own nature—a nature that was sinful. This sinful nature is at war with God. Paul wrote:

> For the sinful nature is always hostile to God. It never did obey God's laws, and it never will (Romans 8:7 NLT).

Although believers have a new nature, the old sinful nature, or the flesh, remains. There is a constant battle between our new nature, and the old sin nature.

Thankfully, Jesus Christ has defeated the power that the old nature has to control the believer. Consequently, Christians do not have to tolerate sin in their lives.

The Apostle Paul wrote about his old nature:

> What a miserable person I am! Who will rescue me from my dying body? I thank God that our Lord Jesus Christ rescues me! So I am obedient to God's standards with my mind, but I am obedient to sin's standards with my corrupt nature (Romans 7:24, 25 God's Word).

The flesh, or old nature, will be with us until we see Christ face-to-face. It is something which we have to endure.

ENEMY NUMBER 3: THE DEVIL

The devil, or Satan, is a personal being who attempts to lure Christians away from Christ. He is an enemy that we all face. Peter warned us about him:

> Keep your mind clear, and be alert. Your opponent the devil is prowling around like a roaring lion as he looks for someone to devour (1 Peter 5:8 God's Word).

Before people trust Jesus Christ as Savior, Satan has a legal claim on them. In fact, they are his slaves until they put their faith in Christ. The Bible speaks of people being in the trap of the devil:

> Then they will come to their senses and escape from the Devil's trap. For they have been held captive by him to do whatever he wants (2 Timothy 2:26 NLT).

Consequently, he presently has a spiritual blindfold over those who are lost. Paul explained this in his second letter to the Corinthians. He wrote:

> If the Good News we preach is veiled from anyone, it is a sign that they are perishing. Satan, the god of this evil world, has blinded the minds of those who don't believe, so they are unable to see the glorious light of the Good News that is shining upon them. They don't understand the message we preach about the glory of Christ, who is the exact likeness of God (2 Corinthians 4:3,4 NLT).

The unbelievers are blind spiritually. They will remain in such a state until their spiritual eyes are opened through faith in Jesus Christ.

CHRIST IS THE VICTOR OVER THE DEVIL

However, Christ has bought each believer—paying the price with His own death. In fact, He came into this world to destroy the works of the devil. The Bible says:

> But when people keep on sinning, it shows they belong to the Devil, who has been sinning since the beginning. But the Son of God came to destroy these works of the Devil (1 John 3:8 NLT).

Therefore, once we put our faith in Christ we do not belong to the devil any longer. We are under a new Master—Jesus Christ. He now has control over us.

The Bible says the devil is powerless against the believer. The writer to the Hebrews made it clear that the death of Christ accomplished this:

Because God's children are human beings—made of flesh and blood —Jesus also became flesh and blood by being born in human form. For only as a human being could he die, and only by dying could he break the power of the Devil, who had the power of death (Hebrews 2:14 NLT).

The victory of Jesus Christ is absolute—the devil has no more power over believers. Jesus has secured victory over the devil.

Scripture has much to say about the devil, his evil angels and demons. We have dedicated two entire books to dealing with these issues: *Evil Angels, Demons and the Occult,* and *Satan.*

WE ARE IN A SPIRITUAL BATTLE

It is clear that believers are in a spiritual battle with the world, the flesh, and the devil. Paul wrote the following to the church at Ephesus:

For we are not fighting against people made of flesh and blood, but against the evil rulers and authorities of the unseen world, against those mighty powers of darkness who rule this world, and against wicked spirits in the heavenly realms. Use every piece of God's armor to resist the enemy in the time of evil, so that after the battle you will still be standing firm (Ephesians 6:12,13 NLT).

Not only are we in a spiritual battle, the weapons that we use are spiritual, not physical. Paul wrote to the Corinthians:

For the weapons of our warfare are not of the flesh but have divine power to destroy strongholds. We destroy arguments and every lofty opinion raised against the knowledge of God, and take every thought captive to obey Christ (2 Corinthians 10:4,5 ESV).

Paul gives the analogy of God's weapons, not worldly weapons, as those that knock down strongholds of the devil. Therefore, we need to understand what weapons we possess in our struggle against our spiritual enemies, and how to use them properly.

THE WEAPONS OF THE BELIEVER

The spiritual weapons of the believer are called the armor of God. Paul explained it this way to the Ephesians:

> For this reason, take up all the armor that God supplies. Then you will be able to take a stand during these evil days. Once you have overcome all obstacles, you will be able to stand your ground. So then, take your stand! Fasten truth around your waist like a belt. Put on God's approval as your breastplate. Put on your shoes so that you are ready to spread the Good News that gives peace. In addition to all these, take the Christian faith as your shield. With it you can put out all the flaming arrows of the evil one. Also take salvation as your helmet and God's word as the sword that the Spirit supplies. Pray in the Spirit in every situation. Use every kind of prayer and request there is. For the same reason be alert. Use every kind of effort and make every kind of request for all of God's people (Ephesians 6:13-18 God's Word).

Our weapons include the Word of God and prayer. We must know how to properly use the Word of God in our struggle with our three enemies. Also, it is necessary that we use the power of prayer to defeat these evil forces that want us to fail.

Again, the good news is that Jesus Christ is the "Victor." Because He is in us, and we are in Him, we can have victory over the world, the flesh, and the devil.

SUMMARY TO QUESTION 1
WHO ARE THE BELIEVER'S ENEMIES? (THE WORLD, THE FLESH, THE DEVIL)

While believers wait for the return of Jesus Christ to the earth, we have to live in a fallen world. In this world we have three main enemies to deal with—the world, the flesh, and the devil. These enemies are all trying to hinder our Christian conduct. We need to be aware of who they are, and how they operate.

The world is the present, sinful, world system. It operates as though God does not exist. It attempts to get believers to participate in an ungodly lifestyle. It is an enemy which Christians must constantly deal with.

The flesh is the sinful nature that each of us is born with. It is not possible for this nature to please God. While Christians have received a new nature, their old nature remains with them. Consequently, there is a constant struggle between these two natures.

The devil is a personal being who is the chief enemy of the Lord. He has ownership of those who are not Christians. He has them in his own trap.

However, once a person comes to Christ by faith, they become a child of God. The devil no longer has any power or authority over them— they now belong to Jesus. Jesus Christ won the victory over the devil by His death on the cross. The power of the devil has been defeated once-and-for-all.

The believer is locked in a struggle with these three enemies. It is a titanic spiritual battle. The weapons that we use to fight this battle are spiritual, not physical. Scripture compares our spiritual weapons to armor.

The key parts of our armor are the Word of God and prayer. This is how our enemies are defeated. The good news is that Jesus has defeated them, and we can also if we place our trust in Him.

What Is the Present World System?
Can the Believer Defend against Worldliness?

The word "world" is a translation of the Greek word *kosmos.* The word basically means "a system characterized by order." We have transliterated that into English with the word "cosmos" meaning "universe." Often in Scripture, it has the meaning of the present world system.

SATAN IS THE RULER OF THIS WORLD SYSTEM

The Bible states that the devil, or Satan, is the ruler of this present world system. When Jesus was tempted by the devil, the kingdoms of the world were offered to Him. Matthew records the following:

> Next the devil took him to the peak of a very high mountain and showed him all the kingdoms of the world and their glory. "I will give it all to you," he said, "if you will kneel down and worship me" (Matthew 4:8,9 NLT).

Jesus acknowledged that Satan was the ruler of this world. Although Jesus did not worship the devil, the Lord did not deny that Satan had the control of the kingdoms of the world.

In the Gospel of John, John records Jesus saying:

The time for judging this world has come, when Satan, the ruler of this world, will be cast out (John 12:31 NLT).

Satan is called the ruler of this world.

In another place in the Gospel of John, Jesus again called Satan the "ruler of this world." We read about it in this manner:

The ruler of this world has no power over me. But he's coming, so I won't talk with you much longer (John 14:30 God's Word).

Satan is the ruler of this present world system. Jesus acknowledged that.

JESUS' KINGDOM IS NOT OF THIS WORLD SYSTEM

There is something else which is important to understand. Jesus declared that His kingdom is not of this present world system. When on trial before Pontius Pilate, we read Jesus saying the following about His kingdom:

My kingdom is not of this world. If it were, my servants would fight to prevent my arrest by the Jews. But now my kingdom is from another place (John 18:36 NLT).

The present world system is characterized by greed, power, selfishness, pleasure, and an external form of religion. In fact, it is ungodly in all of its forms.

HOW TO DEFEND AGAINST WORLDLINESS

Worldliness may be defined as enjoying our participation in this present world system to the place where we neglect the things of God. Worldliness attempts to pull us away from our first love—God.

There are certain things believers can do to defend against, and prevent, worldliness from affecting them.

WE SHOULD NOT BE FRIENDLY TO THE WORLD

The Bible tells us not to befriend this evil world system, which, by its very nature, does not promote the things of God. James wrote:

> You adulterous people! Don't you know that friendship with the world is hostility toward God? So whoever wants to be the friend of the world becomes the enemy of God (James 4:4 CSB).

Believers are not to be friends of this world. Indeed, friends of this world system show themselves to be enemies with God.

WE SHOULD REFUSE TO BE MOLDED TO THE WORLD

The Christian can defend against worldliness by turning themselves over to God and refusing to be molded to our present world system. Paul wrote:

> Therefore, brothers and sisters, in view of the mercies of God, I urge you to present your bodies as a living sacrifice, holy and pleasing to God; this is your true worship. Do not be conformed to this age, but be transformed by the renewing of your mind, so that you may discern what is the good, pleasing, and perfect will of God (Romans 12:1-2 CSB).

We are not to be conformed to this present age, or this present world. Instead we are to be transformed in our thinking.

John states the matter about as clear as it can be stated: if we love this world system, then the love of God the Father is not in us:

> Do not love the world or the things in the world. If anyone loves the world, the love of the Father is not in him (1 John 2:15 NKJV).

We, as believers, do not want to be guilty of loving this present world order.

WE SHOULD BE LOOKING FOR HIS RETURN

Scripture says that we are to deny worldly lust, or desire, by keeping our excitement centered on the return of Christ. Paul wrote to Titus:

> For the grace of God has appeared, bringing salvation for all people, instructing us to deny godlessness and worldly lusts and to live in a sensible, righteous, and godly way in the present age, while we wait for the blessed hope, the appearing of the glory of our great God and Savior, Jesus Christ. He gave himself for us to redeem us from all lawlessness and to cleanse for himself a people for his own possession, eager to do good works (Titus 2:11-14 CSB).

If our minds are centered on Jesus Christ, His kingdom, and His return to earth, then the things of this world will not be attractive to us. Indeed, how could they be? There is really no comparison between the two.

4. WE ARE TO USE BUT NOT TO ABUSE THE WORLD SYSTEM

The Bible says that we, as believers in Jesus Christ, are to use the world but not abuse it. Paul wrote to the Corinthians:

> Those in frequent contact with the things of the world should make good use of them without becoming attached to them, for this world and all it contains will pass away (1 Corinthians 7:31 NLT).

We have to live in this present world system, this is a fact. Yet we do not have to wrongly use it. Indeed, we have a choice in how we will deal with this evil world.

WE SHOULD REMAIN ALOOF TO THE WORLD

We should maintain an attitude of aloofness to the world. James wrote about the necessity to keep ourselves unspotted from the world:

> Pure, unstained religion, according to God our Father, is to take care of orphans and widows when they suffer and to remain uncorrupted by this world (James 1:27 God's Word).

We should be separate from the world system in our desires, motives, and actions. This does not mean that we stop all contact with the world, the idea is that we do not conform ourselves to it.

THERE ARE BENEFITS IF WE SEPARATE OURSELVES FROM THE WORLD

There are a number of benefits to be had when we separate ourselves from the world. For one thing, Paul wrote that God would act like a Father toward us:

> The Lord says, "Get away from unbelievers. Separate yourselves from them. Have nothing to do with anything unclean. Then I will welcome you." The Lord Almighty says, "I will be your Father, and you will be my sons and daughters." (2 Corinthians 6:17,18 God's Word).

When we are rejected by this world system, we are embraced by God the Father.

There is also the possibility of unhindered communion with the Lord when we refuse to be a part of the evil world system. The writer to the Hebrews said:

> So we must go to him outside the camp and endure the insults he endured. We don't have a permanent city here on earth, but we are looking for the city that we will have in the future. Through Jesus we should always bring God a sacrifice of praise, that is, words that acknowledge him (Hebrews 13:13–15 God's Word).

By rejecting the world system, we will bear spiritual fruit. Paul wrote to Titus about some of the benefits of keeping oneself unspotted from the world:

Those who stop associating with dishonorable people will be honored. They will be set apart for the master's use, prepared to do good things (2 Timothy 2:21 God's Word).

When we conform to the present world system, then we lose all of these benefits which Christ offers. Though we do not lose our salvation, we do lose our witness for Jesus Christ.

WE CAN TRUST CHRIST TO GIVE US THE VICTORY OVER THE WORLD

Jesus Christ has made it possible for the believer to have victory over this present world system. John wrote:

> To love God means that we obey his commandments. Obeying his commandments isn't difficult because everyone who has been born from God has won the victory over the world. Our faith is what wins the victory over the world (1 John 5:3,4 God's Word).

Therefore, we can rely on the promise of God that, through Jesus Christ, we can defeat the world system that is trying to make us conform to its ungodly ways. We can overcome the world through Christ.

Consequently, it is important that we understand the present world system—one of our enemies—as well as how we can spiritually defeat it. Thankfully, Scripture tells us how victory can be accomplished.

SUMMARY TO QUESTION 2
WHAT IS THE PRESENT WORLD SYSTEM? HOW CAN THE BELIEVER DEFEND AGAINST WORLDLINESS?

Scripture says that those who have trusted Christ are confronted with three major enemies. One of the enemies of the believer is what is known as the world—this present world system. It is a system which is characterized by selfishness and greed.

Believers are told not to love the present world system. Indeed, if we love this world, then we are told in Scripture that the love of the Father is not in us.

Though we have to live in this present world, it is not our home. However, because we do have to live in it, we must be careful not to fall into the temptation of worldliness.

This consists of enjoying our participation in the world to the place where we neglect the things of the Lord. This is something which we are commanded not to do.

The good news is that there are a number of measures that can be taken to defend against worldliness. They include the following:

First, the believer should not be friendly with this world—the world system is our enemy; therefore, we should treat it in this manner. We should detest everything in this ungodly world system which is against all things biblical.

In addition, the believer in Jesus Christ should refuse to be molded into the present ungodly world system. Indeed, we do not belong to this system. In fact, our citizenship is in heaven. Thus, we should not act as though we do belong.

One of the best antidotes for worldliness is looking forward to the return of Jesus Christ. This keeps our minds set on the things of God.

We must live in this world, but we should not abuse it. There should be an attitude of aloofness to the world. It is not our home.

There are a number of benefits for the believer when we reject worldliness. They can be summed up as follows:

First, God has promised to act like a Father to those who refuse to conform to the present world system. When the world rejects us, we are accepted by the Father.

There is also the promise of unhindered communion with the Lord when we turn away from this sinful world.

In addition, we will bear spiritual fruit for the kingdom. This is another benefit of rejecting worldliness.

Finally, we can trust in the promise of God that Jesus Christ has given us victory over this world system. By trusting Him, we can remain unspotted from this world which acts as though God does not exist.

How Does God Feel about Earthly Success?

Is earthly success something that Scripture frowns upon? Is it more in keeping with Christ's commandments to be poor?

Throughout the history of the church, there have been those who have felt that poverty is equated with spirituality. However, this is not what the Scripture teaches. From the Bible, we can learn the following about the proper attitude toward riches.

1. BELIEVERS SHOULD NOT LOVE MONEY

It is not riches itself that are evil, but rather the love of money. Paul wrote the following to Timothy about what money can do to people:

> For the love of money is the root of all kinds of evil. And some people, craving money, have wandered from the true faith and pierced themselves with many sorrows (1 Timothy 6:10 NLT).

Riches are neutral. They are not good or bad in and of themselves. It all depends upon how we use them. However, it is clear that the love of money can lead to all sorts of evil.

ANYTHING WE POSSESS IS ONLY TEMPORARY

Anything we possess in this life is only temporary. We come into this world with nothing, and we certainly leave it with nothing. The Apostle Paul explained it in this manner:

> After all, we didn't bring anything with us when we came into the world, and we certainly cannot carry anything with us when we die (1 Timothy 6:7 NLT).

Since we cannot take anything with us, we should attempt to work for things that do not perish. Jesus said that we should be concerned with the eternal, not the temporal. Jesus said:

> I tell you the truth, you want to be with me because I fed you, not because you understood the miraculous signs. But don't be so concerned about perishable things like food. Spend your energy seeking the eternal life that the Son of Man can give you. For God the Father has given me the seal of his approval (John 6:26,27 NLT).

The Bible reminds us that anything we possess in this life has only temporary value. Therefore, we should place our attention on the things which are eternal, not temporal. Indeed, the things of this world will eventually pass away.

JESUS STRESSED WHAT IS REALLY IMPORTANT

Jesus stressed what is really important, and what is not. In Luke, we read of Him saying that our lives consist of more than our possessions:

> He then told them, "Watch out and be on guard against all greed, because one's life is not in the abundance of his possessions" (Luke 12:15 CSB).

Our success in life is not to be equated with our possessions. Indeed, earthly success, or riches, does not necessarily mean that the Lord is blessing us.

THE ACCOUNT OF A RICH YOUNG RULER

The New Testament relates the story of an encounter between Jesus and a rich young ruler. Jesus realized that this man's possessions meant very much to him. In fact, they kept him from following after Christ.

Consequently, Jesus told him to sell all his possessions and give them to the poor. However, he could not do it. We then read what happened:

> But he was sad at this word, and went away sorrowful, for he had great possessions (Mark 10:22 NKJV).

This wealthy man was not willing to give up his riches to follow Christ. This remains true of many people today.

5. WE SHOULD STORE UP RICHES IN HEAVEN

The riches that we want to store up should be in heaven. Jesus informed us where to find real riches:

> Don't store up treasures here on earth, where they can be eaten by moths and get rusty, and where thieves break in and steal. Store your treasures in heaven, where they will never become moth-eaten or rusty and where they will be safe from thieves. Wherever your treasure is, there your heart and thoughts will also be (Matthew 6:19-21 NLT).

Heaven is the place of true riches. Above all, it should be our desire to have riches in heaven. If this is the case, then we will conduct our lives accordingly.

Ultimately, our goal should be to please God in every aspect of our lives —it is not merely to gain riches here upon the earth. Earthly success should not be our main goal in life.

SUMMARY TO QUESTION 3
HOW DOES GOD FEEL ABOUT EARTHLY SUCCESS?

The world system in which we live is not our ultimate home. Scripture stresses this truth. Does this mean the Lord wants all believers to be poor? There have been those in the history of the church who have thought so.

Yet Scripture teaches that money is neutral—it is neither good nor bad. Thus, it is not a sin for Christians to be wealthy. What is wrong is the *love* of money, for it may lead to all types of evil.

The key is to have the proper perspective. Any success in this world is only temporary. We certainly cannot bring our money with us into the next world. Since we enter the world with nothing, and leave with nothing, our hearts should be set on things other than worldly riches, or earthly success.

Jesus stressed what is important—the eternal things. We ought to have the same view as He Himself expressed. Our lives consist of more than what we possess.

This being the case, our goal should be to store up riches where it really counts—heaven. Ultimately, any earthly success will not matter. It will only be those treasures which we have stored up in heaven that will have any meaning. This is what we should set our affections upon, not some type of earthly success.

How Is a Christian Supposed to Participate in the World?

We have no choice but to live in this world. Since believers have to live in this godless world system, what are the things that we should, and should not, do? What does the Bible say?

There are a number of points which need to be made.

BELIEVERS ARE FOREIGNERS IN THIS WORLD – THIS IS NOT OUR HOME

To begin with, we must always remember that this present world is not our real home. Peter made this clear when he wrote:

> From Peter, an apostle of Jesus Christ. To God's people who are scattered like foreigners in Pontus, Galatia, Cappadocia, Asia, and Bithynia (1 Peter 1:1 CEV).

We are called foreigners in this world. This world system is not the home of the believer in Jesus Christ. Consequently, we should not live our lives as though we will be living here forever.

BELIEVERS HAVE BEEN SENT INTO THE WORLD

While this world is not our home, this is where we do God's work. Jesus, in His prayer to God the Father, said that believers have been sent into the world to be His representatives.

John records Him praying the following:

> As you sent me into the world, I also have sent them into the world (John 17:18 CSB).

As Jesus was sent by God the Father, believers are also sent to do a job for God. This is why we are in the world. We should never forget this.

3. BELIEVERS MUST MAINTAIN GOOD WORKS

While we are living in this present world, it is our responsibility to maintain good works. Paul emphasized this when he wrote to Titus. He put it this way:

> This saying is trustworthy. I want you to insist on these things, so that those who have believed God might be careful to devote themselves to good works. These are good and profitable for everyone (Titus 3:8 CSB).

Notice that he said that we should be devoted to good works. We are to do the things which are beneficial to everyone.

In another place, Paul again wrote about the importance of doing that which is good to everyone. He said this to the Galatians:

> Whenever we have the opportunity, we have to do what is good for everyone, especially for the family of believers (Galatians 6:10 God's Word).

We are to imitate Christ in doing good things. Therefore, as He did good things while in this world, believers, in imitating Him, should do likewise.

4. WE SHOULD BE THE LIGHT OF THE WORLD

Jesus commanded those of us who follow Him to let our light shine while we are in this world. In the Sermon on the Mount, we read of Him saying:

> You are the light of the world—like a city on a mountain, glowing in the night for all to see. Don't hide your light under a basket! Instead, put it on a stand and let it shine for all. In the same way, let your good deeds shine out for all to see, so that everyone will praise your heavenly Father" (Matthew 5:14-16 NLT).

Light, of course, is used to extinguish darkness. Even when a small light comes into a large room, the light always overpowers the darkness.

Paul wrote to the Ephesians with a similar emphasis. Once we are spiritually awake, Jesus will be our light; He will guide us through the darkness:

> Therefore He says: "Awake, you who sleep, arise from the dead, and Christ will give you light" (Ephesians 5:14 NKJV).

Believers are to shine like lights in a darkened world.

WE SHOULD BE THE SALT OF THE EARTH

We are also told to be the salt of the earth. Again, in the Sermon on the Mount, we read of Jesus' words:

> You are like salt for everyone on earth. But if salt no longer tastes like salt, how can it make food salty? All it is good for is to be thrown out and walked on (Matthew 5:13 CEV).

In Jesus' day, salt was used for a variety of things. For example, it was spread on a field and used as a fertilizer to promote good growth. Salt was also used as a disinfectant to kill off unwanted bugs.

Salt was also used as preservative. It was used with meat and fish to prevent them from decaying.

The Roman soldiers were paid with salt. This is where the English word "salary" is derived.

Consequently, salt had many uses.

SALT AND LIGHT BOTH PENETRATE

What salt and light have in common is penetration. As the salt penetrates the food to preserve it, light penetrates the darkness. The effect is to change the situation for the better.

In the same manner, believers are to penetrate the darkened world with the message of Christ—the light of life. When the freeing message of Jesus Christ enters into a life, that person is changed for the better. Thus, we are to bring light to this darkened world.

To have an impact, Christians must be set apart from the world. This is not something physical. Believers must live and interact within our world, but they must do it without compromising with the world system. Compromise takes the form of both belief and behavior. Indeed, Christians are to have a different belief system than unbelievers, and Christians are to behave consistently with the Scripture—not with what is fashionable with the world.

Paul stressed this important truth in his letter to the Romans. We are to live apart from the actions of this present world system—we are not to think the same way in which the world thinks. We are to be different. He put it this way:

And so, dear brothers and sisters, I plead with you to give your bodies to God. Let them be a living and holy sacrifice - the kind he will accept. When you think of what he has done for you, is this too much to ask? Don't copy the behavior and customs of this world, but let God transform you into a new person by changing the way you think. Then you will know what God wants you to do, and you will know how good and pleasing and perfect his will really is (Romans 12:1,2 NLT)

If we are truly to have an impact in this world, then we are not to compromise our convictions. While we have to live in this world, we must not live like the rest of the people in the world. For the sake of Jesus Christ, we need to think and act differently.

SUMMARY TO QUESTION 4
HOW IS A CHRISTIAN SUPPOSED TO PARTICIPATE IN THE WORLD?

This world system is not the home of the believer. We are called strangers in this world because our real home is with God in the next world. Indeed, Heaven is our home!

However, believers are sent into this present world system to do the Lord's work. We are here to do a job for the Lord. As God the Father sent God the Son into the world to do His work, those who have believed in Christ have been sent to do the work of the Lord.

While in this present world, we need to do good works. Our deeds must glorify the God of the Bible. Scripture commands us to do the works which do glorify God, which make God look good. This is what we should be doing.

We are compared to both salt and light. This means that we are to penetrate into the world system in which we live. We are to have an impact in this world that honors the Lord. We do this by rejecting the values and ideals of this world system, and allow our hearts and minds to be transformed. We need to act like Christ, to think His thoughts.

It is in this manner that believers in Jesus Christ are supposed to participate in the world. If we do so, in this way, then we can have that impact for the Lord which will make our lives worth living.

What Drives a Born-Again Christian to Sin?
(The Old Nature, the Old Man, the Flesh)

Although Christians know the difference between right and wrong, many times they knowingly do what is wrong. Why? Why do Christians break God's rule and sin?

1. WHY A BORN-AGAIN CHRISTIAN IS DRIVEN TO SIN

Part of the reason, as to why Christians are driven to sin, is because it is attractive to us. There is something in our fallen nature, our makeup, that wants to sin. Our sinful actions merely reflect what is on the inside of all of us—the old sinful nature. Jesus made this clear:

> What comes from your heart is what makes you unclean. Out of your heart come evil thoughts, vulgar deeds, stealing, murder, unfaithfulness in marriage, greed, meanness, deceit, indecency, envy, insults, pride, and foolishness (Mark 7:20-22 CEV).

Sin comes from the human heart—our hearts, at the core, are sinful. This is how the Bible describes each and every one of us.

2. SIN IS PLEASURABLE FOR A TIME

The Bible recognizes that sin is pleasurable, but it is only for a short time. We read in Hebrews about the behavior of Moses:

Then after Moses grew up, his faith made him refuse to be called Pharaoh's grandson. He chose to be mistreated with God's people instead of having the good time that sin could bring for a little while (Hebrews 11:24,25 CEV).

Moses made a choice. He reckoned that it was better to suffer with the people of the Lord, instead of experiencing a short time of pleasure from sinning. We should make the same choice.

3. THERE IS AN ONGOING INNER STRUGGLE IN OUR INNERMOST BEING

The Apostle Paul, the greatest missionary in Christian history, had a struggle with the sin that was inside of him. He discovered that he often did the things he did not want to do, and that he didn't do the things which he wanted to do. He wrote of this struggle in his letter to the Romans. He put it this way:

> In fact, I don't understand why I act the way I do. I don't do what I know is right. I do the things I hate. Although I don't do what I know is right, I agree that the Law is good. So I am not the one doing these evil things. The sin that lives in me is what does them. I know that my selfish desires won't let me do anything that is good. Even when I want to do right, I cannot. Instead of doing what I know is right, I do wrong. And so, if I don't do what I know is right, I am no longer the one doing these evil things. The sin that lives in me is what does them (Romans 7:15-20 CEV).

Each and every believer can identify with Paul here. Indeed, the struggle of Paul is also our struggle. While we may want to do that which is right, for some reason, we do not always do this. The sin, that is inside us, fights against the Spirit.

Furthermore, this struggle is something which is continuous. Indeed, it will continue as long as we are in these mortal bodies.

THE PROBLEM GOES BACK TO ADAM

This problem, as to why we can still be driven to sin, goes all the way back to the Garden of Eden. The Bible says all of us have inherited a sin nature. After the first two human beings, Adam and Eve, sinned, they conceived sons and daughters in their own likeness.

We read the following in Genesis that explains what took place:

> Adam was 130 years old when he fathered a son in his likeness, according to his image, and named him Seth (Genesis 5:3 CSB).

Adam's image, or likeness, means that these children were born with the same nature as Adam—a sinful nature. Since the time of Adam, all of us that have been born have been born with that same sin nature.

This nature is characterized by a tendency to serve self, rather than to serve God. Its tendency is to leave God out of our thoughts, and out of our actions.

This old sin nature of ours is constantly urging, or driving, us to sin. The old sin nature wants to do evil, rather than good. It also wants to do neutral things that exclude God from the picture. In other words, this nature will do whatever it takes to keep us from serving the Lord.

IT IS ALSO CALLED THE "OLD MAN"

In some translations of Scripture, the old sin nature is known as the "old man" with the new nature being described as the "new man." Paul wrote:

> Knowing this, that our old man was crucified with *Him,* that the body of sin might be done away with, that we should no longer be slaves of sin (Romans 6:6 NKJV).

The old man is the human nature that each of us was born with. It has no capacity to please God. None. Neither can the old nature understand spiritual things. Paul wrote that without the Spirit of God, spiritual things will be viewed as foolish. He said:

> But the person without the Spirit does not receive what comes from God's Spirit, because it is foolishness to him; he is not able to understand it since it is evaluated spiritually (1 Corinthians 2:14 CSB).

Those who have not become Christians only have the capacity to serve self. The old nature is always bad, and it cannot be improved. At the basis of our old nature is the desire to manage our lives by ourselves. It does not allow any room for God to lead us, or to control our life. It is totally self-centered. This is why it likes to sin.

THE "FLESH"

The Bible speaks about the "flesh." The flesh is a term that is used in Scripture a number of different ways. At times, it refers to the entire composition of a human being.

However, the flesh is another term for the old sin nature—the nature that is antagonistic against God. Paul wrote:

> For I know that nothing good lives in me, that is, in my flesh. For the desire to do what is good is with me, but there is no ability to do it. (Romans 7:18 CSB).

The mark of a genuine believer is a person who is not living in the flesh, —the old nature—but is led by the Spirit of God. Paul wrote:

> You, however, are not in the flesh, but in the Spirit, if indeed the Spirit of God lives in you. If anyone does not have the Spirit of Christ, he does not belong to him (Romans 8:9 CSB).

Believers are to allow the Holy Spirit to lead them. If we do this, then we will not practice sin.

In sum, Christians are driven to sin because of this old sinful nature which resides in each one of us. It is an ongoing battle. Only the leading of God the Holy Spirit will allow us to win the victory over sin. Thus, we must allow Him to guide us in all things.

SUMMARY TO QUESTION 5
WHAT DRIVES A BORN-AGAIN CHRISTIAN TO SIN? (THE OLD NATURE, THE OLD MAN, THE FLESH)

Born-again Christians are those who have trusted Jesus Christ for salvation, have turned from sin, and have turned to God. However, Christians still sin. Why is this? What drives a believer to sin?

There are a number of reasons as to why this is so. For one thing, Christians are driven to sin because we are still in a body that has a sinful nature. The Bible recognizes that sin is pleasurable for a time—but it is only a short period of time. Even the Apostle Paul admitted his struggle with the old sin nature. He found that he did not always do the things which he wanted to do.

The Bible says that believers have two natures—an old nature and a new nature. There is a struggle going on inside each of us for control. The old nature wants to sin, while the new natures hates it. Therefore, it should not surprise us when we have sinful desires.

The reason we sin goes back to the inner struggle we all face. From the time that Adam and Eve sinned in the Garden of Eden, everyone has been born with a sinful nature. The Bible calls this nature by a number of different terms. This includes: the old nature, the old man, and the flesh.

A non-Christian operates entirely by the old nature. They are unable to understand spiritual things. While the Christian inherits a new nature, we do not lose our old nature upon believing. Rather, we have a new nature that is able to please God. The mark of a genuine, born-again believer is one who is led by the new nature. Yet, the old nature is always there, trying to keep us from allowing the new nature to guide us.

This is why we have the struggle, and this is why we sin. The old nature wants to get the victory over the new nature.

However, it does not have to be that way. Christ has won the victory over the old sin nature. It does not have to master us any longer. Yet, we have to make the choice to be led by the Holy Spirit, and the new nature.

QUESTION 6

What Is the New Nature?

Prior to salvation in Jesus Christ, we could only serve ourselves. This is the only capacity the non-Christian has. Once a person trusts Christ as Savior, they now have a new nature. However, the old nature does not go away. It will not leave the believer until the Christian goes to heaven.

1. ALL BELIEVERS HAVE A NEW NATURE

The Bible says that all believers receive a new nature upon their trusting Christ as Savior. Furthermore, the new nature that we have, cannot sin. Paul wrote:

> You must display a new nature because you are a new person, created in God's likeness—righteous, holy, and true (Ephesians 4:24 NLT).

The new person is not merely a reformation of the old nature, it is an entirely new person. Paul wrote to the Corinthians:

> Therefore, if anyone is in Christ, he is a new creation; the old has passed away, and see, the new has come! (2 Corinthians 5:17 CSB).

Things have now become new.

Believers are actually partakers of the divine nature. Peter revealed this important truth when he wrote his second letter to the believers. He said:

> God made great and marvelous promises, so that his nature would become part of us. Then we could escape our evil desires and the corrupt influences of this world (2 Peter 1:4 CEV).

The Bible says that we also have the mind of Christ. Paul emphasized this when he wrote to the Corinthians. He put it this way:

> The Scriptures ask, "Has anyone ever known the thoughts of the Lord or given him advice?" But we understand what Christ is thinking (1 Corinthians 2:16 CSB).

This is a wonderful truth—we have the mind of Christ. We can think the same types of things which Christ thinks.

2. THERE IS A CONSTANT STRUGGLE OF THE NATURES

The Bible says that there is a constant struggle between the old and new natures. Scripture states it in this manner:

> If you are guided by the Spirit, you won't obey your selfish desires. The Spirit and your desires are enemies of each other. They are always fighting each other and keeping you from doing what you feel you should (Galatians 5:16,17 CEV).

Those who live according to the sinful nature have their minds set on what that old nature desires, but those who live in accordance with the Spirit, have their minds set on what the Spirit desires. The mind of sinful humanity is death, but the mind controlled by the Spirit is life and peace. The sinful mind is hostile to God. It does not submit to God's law, nor can it do so.

We are told not to encourage the old nature in any way:

But let the Lord Jesus Christ take control of you, and don't think of ways to indulge your evil desires (Romans 13:14 NLT).

The two natures are in a constant struggle.

3. IT IS A LIFE-LONG STRUGGLE

The struggle between the two natures will continue during the entire life of the believer. Deliverance is by means of the Holy Spirit working through the new nature to hold down strong desires of the old sin nature. This life-long battle will only be over when the believer goes to be with the Lord. Until that time, the battle goes on.

SUMMARY TO QUESTION 6
WHAT IS THE NEW NATURE?

Before a person trusts Christ as Savior, before they become a Christian, they only have the capacity to serve self. They only have one nature—a sin nature.

However, when a person trusts Christ as Savior, they inherit a new nature. The new nature only has the capacity to serve the Lord. Scripture teaches us a number of things about the new nature.

The Bible says that all things have become new to the believer. With our new nature, we have a new outlook on life. We have new desires, new interests, and new goals.

It also says that we are partakers of the divine nature. In some sense, we are able to participate in His nature.

Elsewhere in Scripture, it says that we have the mind of Christ. We can think His thoughts and we can be like Him in a number of ways. All of this is possible because of the new nature.

However, since the old nature still lives within each believer, there is a constant struggle for control. This life-long struggle will continue until the time that believers receive their new bodies. Until then, there is a spiritual struggle going on.

The good news is that the new nature can always have victory over the old. Christ has secured that victory for us. It is our responsibility to let the new nature take over so we can enter into these spiritual victories.

How Can We Defeat the Old Nature? (The Flesh)

Christians still have that old sin nature that resides in them. Although they have been spiritually reborn, they still have this struggle inside. Paul wrote of his own personal struggle in his letter to the Romans. He said the following:

> Oh, what a miserable person I am! Who will free me from this life that is dominated by sin? (Romans 7:24 NLT)

This struggle with sin will continue until all of us receive our new bodies. How then, can we have victory over the old nature?

HOW TO DEFEAT THE OLD NATURE

Defeating the old nature consists of practicing a number of important things. They include the following steps:

REALIZE THE OLD NATURE WAS CRUCIFIED WITH CHRIST

The first step is to realize that the old nature was crucified with Christ—it does not have to rule our lives any longer. Paul taught this to the Galatians:

> I have been crucified with Christ, and I no longer live, but Christ lives in me. The life I now live in the body, I live by

faith in the Son of God, who loved me and gave himself for me (Galatians 2:20 CSB).

The Contemporary English Version puts it this way:

> I have died, but Christ lives in me. And I now live by faith in the Son of God, who loved me and gave his life for me. I don't turn my back on God's undeserved kindness. If we can be acceptable to God by obeying the Law, it was useless for Christ to die (Galatians 2:20 CEV).

We have died with Christ. He now lives in us through the Holy Spirit. Consequently, we always have the capacity to say yes to Him and no to sin.

The old nature does not have any authority over us. Jesus Christ died for the penalty of sin, but He also died to free the believer from the power of sin. The believer does not have to be a slave to sin.

Paul instructed the Romans about what it means to be crucified with Jesus Christ. He explained it in this manner:

> Our old sinful selves were crucified with Christ so that sin might lose its power in our lives. We are no longer slaves to sin. For when we died with Christ we were set free from the power of sin. And since we died with Christ, we know we will also share his new life. We are sure of this because Christ rose from the dead, and he will never die again. Death no longer has any power over him. He died once to defeat sin, and now he lives for the glory of God (Romans 6:6-10 NLT).

Note that Paul said our sinful selves have been crucified with Jesus Christ. Therefore, sin does not have any power, or authority, over us. Indeed, we are dead to sin, but alive to God. We have been set free! What a marvelous truth!

Paul wrote elsewhere to the Romans about the freedom which believers now have through Jesus Christ. He said:

> For the power of the life-giving Spirit has freed you through Christ Jesus from the power of sin that leads to death. The law of Moses could not save us, because of our sinful nature. But God put into effect a different plan to save us. He sent his own Son in a human body like ours, except that ours are sinful. God destroyed sin's control over us by giving his Son as a sacrifice for our sins. He did this so that the requirement of the law would be fully accomplished for us who no longer follow our sinful nature but instead follow the Spirit (Romans 8:2-4 NLT).

The good news is that Jesus has set us free. We do not have to be enslaved any longer to our old selfish desires. We can live in newness of life in Christ.

2. WE ARE TO WALK IN THE NEW NATURE

While we have been crucified with Jesus Christ, the believer will always have to live with this old nature—until our bodies are changed. Scripture thus commands us not to walk in the flesh, but in the Spirit.

To walk in the Spirit is to overcome the flesh. This is how we please God. On the other hand, those who live a lifestyle in the flesh cannot please God. Paul made this very clear in his words to the Romans:

> That's why those who are still under the control of their sinful nature can never please God (Romans 8:8 NLT).

The Christian, led by the Spirit, can please the Lord. Indeed, the spiritual Christian wants to please the Lord in the way in which they live.

Paul wrote to the Galatians about the necessity of being led by the Spirit of God. He compared the two natures which are in opposition.

He showed what it means to live in the old nature, as well as what it means to be led with the new nature. He said:

> I say then, walk by the Spirit and you will certainly not carry out the desire of the flesh. For the flesh desires what is against the Spirit, and the Spirit desires what is against the flesh; these are opposed to each other, so that you don't do what you want. But if you are led by the Spirit, you are not under the law (Galatians 5:16-18 CSB).

The believer is to thus walk in the Spirit to produce the fruit of the Spirit. In doing so, we will not gratify the desires of the old nature, the flesh. This is how we are supposed to live.

WE SHOULD CONTINUOUSLY EXAMINE OURSELVES IN LIGHT OF GOD'S WORD

To defeat the old sin nature, we must be continuously examining our lives to determine who is actually guiding us. Is it the old nature or the new nature? It is important that we know.

The psalmist wrote:

> Examine me, and probe my thoughts! Test me, and know my concerns! See if there is any idolatrous tendency in me, and lead me in the reliable ancient path! (Psalm 139:23,24 NET).

Believers should be in a continuous state of examining themselves. We should never take it for granted that it is the Spirit of God who is leading us.

WE MUST CONFESS OUR SINS WHEN WE BECOME AWARE OF THEM

Even when we live according to the Spirit we still sin. When the Lord shows us our sin, we should immediately confess it to Him. John wrote about the necessity of confession of sin before the Lord. He said:

If we confess our sins, he is faithful and righteous to forgive us our sins and to cleanse us from all unrighteousness (1 John 1:9 CSB).

It is important that we confess our sins when we become aware of them. This is how we will continue to be led by the Spirit.

WE NEED TO TRUST GOD THAT OUR SINS ARE FORGIVEN

Next, we must trust God's promise that our sins have been forgiven. This means that we believe what His Word says. John wrote that we are able to know that we have eternal life because of Jesus Christ. He stated it this way:

And this is the testimony: God has given us eternal life, and this life is in his Son. The one who has the Son has life. The one who does not have the Son of God does not have life. I have written these things to you who believe in the name of the Son of God so that you may know that you have eternal life (1 John 5:11-13 CSB).

Believers in Jesus Christ can *know* that they have eternal life, they can *know* that their sins have been forgiven. This is something that each believer can be assured of.

WE NEED TO STARVE THE OLD NATURE AND FEED THE NEW NATURE

The best remedy, for defeating the old nature, is to starve it and feed the new nature. Paul wrote to the Philippians about the need to think about godly things:

Finally brothers and sisters, whatever is true, whatever is honorable, whatever is just, whatever is pure, whatever is lovely, whatever is commendable—if there is any moral excellence and if there is anything praiseworthy—dwell on these things (Philippians 4:8 CSB).

These are the things which we must constantly think about.

Paul wrote to the Romans about the need to put off the old life and put on the new. He stated it this way:

> The night is nearly over, and the day is near; so let us discard the deeds of darkness and put on the armor of light. Let us walk with decency, as in the daytime: not in carousing and drunkenness; not in sexual impurity and promiscuity; not in quarreling and jealousy. But put on the Lord Jesus Christ, and don't make plans to gratify the desires of the flesh (Romans 13:12-14 CSB).

If we want to defeat the old nature, we need to apply all these things to our lives. Victory can be ours!

SUMMARY TO QUESTION 7
HOW CAN WE DEFEAT THE OLD NATURE? (THE FLESH)

Our desire, as Christians, should be to defeat the old nature—the flesh. Indeed, this should be the goal of every Bible-believer.

The bad news is that the old nature resides in every Christian. The good news is that it can be defeated because of what Christ has done for us. There are a number of steps which we must take.

First, we must realize that our old self was crucified with Jesus Christ—it does not have to live any longer. This is very good news!

Second, we should walk in the new nature that we have been given. The spiritual Christian lives their life by means of the Holy Spirit, and not our own sinful desires. By the guidance of the Spirit of God, we are able to live a life which is pleasing to Him.

However, we also must continuously examine ourselves in the light of the Word of God, to make certain that we are walking by means of the Spirit. We cannot take for granted that we are always doing the things pleasing to Him.

Consequently, a continuous examination is necessary. Even with all of this, we will still sin. When we sin, we need to immediately confess it. We acknowledge our failures, and then move on.

Trusting God that our sins are forgiven is something else we should do. We do not wallow in our past sins. They have been forgiven and forgotten.

Finally, we must continually starve the old nature, and feed the new nature. If we do all of these things, and keep doing them, then we can defeat the old nature.

Who Is the Natural Man?
(The Natural Person)

The Bible speaks of a person known as the "natural man" or "natural person." There are a number of things that the Bible says about this type of person. It is important that we understand exactly what is taught.

1. THE NATURAL PERSON IS AN UNBELIEVER

To begin with, we find that the Bible speaks of the natural person as one who has not received Jesus Christ as their Savior. In other words, these people are still lost in sin. Paul contrasts this type of person with those who know Christ:

> Every word we speak was taught to us by God's Spirit, not by human wisdom. And this same Spirit helps us teach spiritual things to spiritual people. That's why only someone who has God's Spirit can understand spiritual blessings. Anyone who doesn't have God's Spirit thinks these blessings are foolish (1 Corinthians 2:13,14 CEV).

This type of individual does not know Jesus Christ. They are not His children. Therefore, the things of God are foolishness to them.

THE NATURAL PERSON OPERATES ON HUMAN WISDOM

There is something else we learn. The natural man, or the natural person, may be defined as an individual who operates entirely on human wisdom. This is due to the fact that they have not made a commitment to Jesus Christ. They have not experienced the new birth, and do not have the Holy Spirit living inside of them.

Because the natural person does not have the Spirit of God living in them, they do not understand, or welcome, spiritual truth. It is all foolishness unto them. Indeed, the unbeliever cannot understand how a person who died 1,900 years ago can have any meaning with the way they are living today. There is no understanding whatsoever.

3. THE NATURAL PERSON HAS NO REAL UNDERSTANDING OF BIBLE

In addition, the natural person does not receive, or welcome, the message of Scripture. Their reaction to the message of the gospel is that it is foolishness, or ridiculous.

Paul wrote about such people when he addressed the church in Corinth. He described these people as follows:

> For it is written, "*I will destroy the wisdom of the wise, and I will thwart the cleverness of the intelligent.*" Where is the wise man? Where is the expert in the Mosaic law? Where is the debater of this age? Has God not made the wisdom of the world foolish? For since in the wisdom of God, the world by its wisdom did not know God, God was pleased to save those who believe by the foolishness of preaching. For Jews demand miraculous signs and Greeks ask for wisdom, but we preach about a crucified Christ, a stumbling block to Jews and foolishness to Gentiles. But to those who are called, both Jews and Greeks, Christ is the power of God and the wisdom of God (1 Corinthians 1:19-24 NET).

Paul makes it clear that these people think the Christian message is foolish; it makes no sense whatsoever to them.

On the other hand, while the natural person sees the Bible as foolish, the Bible says that the wisdom of this world system is foolishness to God.

4. THE NATURAL PERSON DOES NOT HAVE THE PROPER EQUIPMENT TO UNDERSTAND SPIRITUAL THINGS

Unsaved humanity does not have the right equipment to make a proper estimate of spiritual truth. As stars are telescopically discerned, and germs are microscopically discerned, the Bible is discerned by the Holy Spirit.

Therefore, we can compare their lack of spiritually ability to a blind person judging an art contest, they have no point of reference. The same holds true for the natural person and spiritual things, there is no reference point.

5. THE NATURAL PERSON HAS A SPIRITUAL BLINDFOLD ON

The Bible also says the unbeliever cannot see spiritual things because they have on a spiritual blindfold. Paul wrote to the Corinthians about the darkness which unbelievers find themselves. He explained it in this manner:

> But if our gospel is veiled, it is veiled to those who are perishing. In their case, the god of this age has blinded the minds of the unbelievers to keep them from seeing the light of the gospel of the glory of Christ, who is the image of God (2 Corinthians 4:3,4 CSB).

Consequently, they cannot understand spiritual things because there is a satanic blindfold covering their eyes.

6. THE NATURAL PERSON MISSES THE PURPOSE OF THE BIBLE

There are many sincere and educated people who admire the Bible as literature. They believe that its moral teachings are among the best that have even been delivered. However, these people miss the real spiritual message of the Bible—that salvation is only through the Person of Jesus Christ. There is no other way in which anyone can be saved.

These same people may acknowledge Christ as a wonderful teacher, or as an example concerning how we should live; yet, they miss the real purpose of why He came into the world.

When Paul wrote to Timothy, he made it plain as to the exact reason Christ did enter our world:

> Christ Jesus came into the world to save sinners. This saying is true, and it can be trusted. I was the worst sinner of all! (1 Timothy 1:15 CEV).

Jesus Christ came into the world to save sinners. Unfortunately, this message is lost upon the "natural person."

This sums up what we know from Scripture about the person who has not yet received Jesus Christ as their Savior, the natural person.

SUMMARY TO QUESTION 8
WHO IS THE NATURAL MAN? (THE NATURAL PERSON)

The Bible speaks of people called "the natural man," or "the natural person." The natural man, or the natural person, is the way the Bible describes an unbeliever. This person operates entirely upon human wisdom. Indeed, they do not understand how the message of the Bible is relevant for them today.

In fact, the gospel message seems completely foolish to them. This is because they do not have the proper equipment to judge spiritual things. The Holy Spirit of God does not indwell these people. Thus, they are not capable of understanding things of the Spirit.

Furthermore, the Scripture says that they have a spiritual blindfold on that keeps them from understanding the things of God. Satan, the god of this age, has blindfolded them to the truths of God.

Consequently, they miss the main purpose of Scripture—the fact that Jesus Christ has come into the world to offer salvation from sin.

The good news is that there is hope for this type of person. Indeed, once they turn to Jesus Christ as Savior, the spiritual blindfold is removed. They can now see things in the way in which God sees them. In other words, they can now see spiritually.

Who Is the Spiritual Man?
(The Spiritual Person)

The Bible speaks of the "natural man" or the "natural person" as one who cannot please God. However, the Bible also speaks of someone known as the "spiritual man" or the "spiritual person." In contrast to the "natural man," this person is able to please the Lord.

Only those who have believed in Jesus Christ qualify as a "spiritual man" or "spiritual person." Scripture says the following about this type of individual.

THE SPIRITUAL PERSON IS IN CONTRAST TO THE NATURAL PERSON

In contrast to the natural person, is the spiritual person. When Paul wrote to the Corinthians he acknowledged the existence of the spiritual person. He put it this way:

> The spiritual person, however, can evaluate everything, yet he himself cannot be evaluated by anyone (1 Corinthians 2:15 CSB).

We find out something about the spiritual person in this passage. They are able to understand and evaluate spiritual truth. In fact, it is only the spiritual person who has this capacity.

THE SPIRITUAL PERSON IS LED BY THE HOLY SPIRIT

There is something else which we discover. The spiritual person is one who is characterized by the leading of the Holy Spirit. In other words, the spiritual person allows the Spirit of God to lead them.

The Bible does indeed command believers to let the Spirit lead them. Paul wrote the following to the Ephesians:

Don't get drunk on wine, which leads to wild living. Instead, be filled with the Spirit by reciting psalms, hymns, and spiritual songs for your own good. Sing and make music to the Lord with your hearts. Always thank God the Father for everything in the name of our Lord Jesus Christ (Ephesians 5:18-20 God's Word).

Only the spiritual person can be led by the Holy Spirit. The natural person, or an unbeliever, has no such capacity.

3. THE SPIRITUAL PERSON PRODUCES THE FRUIT OF THE SPIRIT

The spiritual person produces the fruit of the Spirit. This is the outward evidence that they have believed in Jesus Christ. When he wrote to the Galatians, the Apostle Paul explained some of the outward results which accompany being led by the Spirit. These fruits can be listed as follows:

> God's Spirit makes us loving, happy, peaceful, patient, kind, good, faithful (Galatians 5:22 CEV).

Only the spiritual person can do this; the natural person has no capacity to know God, to please God, or to serve God. None whatsoever!

SUMMARY TO QUESTION 9
WHO IS THE SPIRITUAL MAN? (THE SPIRITUAL PERSON)

The Bible contrasts the "spiritual man" or "spiritual person" with the "natural man" or "natural person." There is such as a person as a natural man, and there is such a person as a spiritual man. The spiritual man is a believer in Jesus Christ.

Among other things, the spiritual man has the capacity to understand spiritual things. Since the Holy Spirit lives inside the spiritual person, we are able to comprehend and evaluate spiritual matters.

In contrast to the spiritual person is the natural person. They do not have any ability to understand the things of the Spirit. Spiritual truth makes no sense to them whatsoever. In other words, the natural person is deaf, and mute, to the things of God. They do not make any sense to that person.

In contrast, the Bible also says that the Holy Spirit leads the spiritual person. He guides their thoughts and behavior. The natural person does not have the Holy Spirit living in them, so they cannot be led by the Spirit. Their thoughts are guided by their own selfish desires. Again, we see the differences between the two.

Finally, the spiritual person is one who can bear spiritual fruit. These qualities include things such as love, joy, and peace. However, this is not possible for the natural person—the unbeliever.

Therefore, we find that the spiritual person has the capacity to please God in all things. The natural person has no such capacity. Consequently, we see the great contrast between the two.

QUESTION 10

What Is the
Carnal Believer?

Scripture speaks of a person known as the "carnal believer." This carnal person is a believer who has not reached spiritual maturity. This individual is controlled by their old sinful nature. They willfully say "Yes" to selfish inclinations, and "No" to the will of God. Their obedience is to their natural appetites, rather than to the things of God. These people have never gone beyond spiritual infancy.

Carnal Christianity is certainly not the ideal. Indeed, the Apostle Paul encouraged the believers to go on to spiritual maturity. He wrote:

> Dear brothers and sisters, when I was with you I couldn't talk to you as I would to mature Christians. I had to talk as though you belonged to this world or as though you were infants in the Christian life. I had to feed you with milk and not with solid food, because you couldn't handle anything stronger. And you still aren't ready, for you are still controlled by your own sinful desires. You are jealous of one another and quarrel with each other. Doesn't that prove you are controlled by your own desires? You are acting like people who don't belong to the Lord (1 Corinthians 3:1-3 NLT).

There is the encouragement for those who believe in Jesus Christ to move on to spiritual maturity. Nobody should remain a spiritual infant, or a carnal Christian.

There are a number of things we learn about this carnal Christian.

THE PERSON'S LIFE IS CHARACTERIZED BY THE OLD NATURE

For one thing, the things of the flesh, or the old sin nature, characterize the actions of the carnal believer. Their old nature, and its sinful appetites, control this person. This is why Paul referred to them as carnal and babes in Christ.

THESE PEOPLE ONLY HAVE A BASIC UNDERSTANDING OF THE BIBLE

The Bible says that the carnal believer understands milk, not solid food. There is a question as to what Paul meant by this. Some say it is a matter of content. Milk is the gospel message and the easier doctrines, while solid food is the harder doctrines such as predictive prophecy.

However, it is probably best to see it as a matter of depth of understanding, not merely the understanding of different doctrines.

The carnal believer restricts themself to the very basics of the faith, and never gets deep into the Word of God. They have no desire to learn anything more than this. This is what characterizes them.

THERE IS A LACK OF GROWTH IN THEIR LIFE

The carnal Christian should have outgrown the baby stage long ago. However, instead of growing, they remain stagnant and unproductive. A Christian who is controlled by the old sin nature does not experience normal growth. Their growth is stunted.

4. THEY OPERATE LIKE UNBELIEVERS

Carnal Christians operate like unbelievers. They behave like the natural, or unsaved, person both internally and externally. Internally they will think and behave like a self-centered person. Their outward behavior will be no different than the unbeliever. Indeed, it is often hard to tell the difference between the two.

Paul spoke of such actions as bringing sorrow to the Holy Spirit:

> And do not bring sorrow to God's Holy Spirit by the way you live. Remember, he is the one who has identified you as his own, guaranteeing that you will be saved on the day of redemption (Ephesians 4:30 NLT).

The Spirit of God is grieved by this sort of behavior.

Consequently, Paul urged the Thessalonians not to quench the spirit—not to put out the Spirit's fire. He wrote:

> Don't put out the Spirit's fire (1 Thessalonians 5:19 God's Word).

A carnal Christian is a walking advertisement for the devil. There is very little in their life that promotes the things of God.

THERE IS A REMEDY FOR THIS CARNALITY

The good news is that there is a remedy for this carnality. The carnal person needs the power of the Holy Spirit to break control of their old sin nature. Since they are acting like unbelievers, this is their only hope. The Holy Spirit is willing to change those desires of the carnal believer, and to guide them into the things of the Lord; however, there must be willingness on the part of the carnal believer to desire godly things.

VICTORY IS AVAILABLE FOR THE CARNAL CHRISTIAN

The good news is that it is possible for the carnal Christian to achieve victory over sin in their life. Three things must happen to accomplish this.

THE CARNAL CHRISTIAN MUST UNDERSTAND THAT CHRIST HAS WON THE VICTORY

First, the carnal Christian must come to understand that Jesus Christ has freed them from the power of sin. Not only did Christ take away the penalty of sin by His death on the cross, He has also freed believers from the bondage of sin. The Bible says:

We know that the person we used to be was crucified with him to put an end to sin in our bodies. Because of this we are no longer slaves to sin. The person who has died has been freed from sin. If we have died with Christ, we believe that we will also live with him (Romans 6:6-8 God's Word).

Victory over sin is possible for the carnal Christian.

THE CARNAL CHRISTIAN MUST TRUST CHRIST TO OVERCOME SIN IN THEIR LIFE

Once the carnal Christian understands what Christ has done for them, the next step is to accept this by faith. They have to personally trust the Lord to help them overcome personal sin, and to live a life that is pleasing to Him.

All of this is possible because of what Jesus accomplished. However, nothing will happen until the person steps out in faith, and trusts God to help them experience the freedom from sin. Paul explained what they must do:

> So put to death the sinful, earthly things lurking within you. Have nothing to do with sexual sin, impurity, lust, and shameful desires. Don't be greedy for the good things of this life, for that is idolatry (Colossians 3:5 NLT).

We should seek after the godly things not the things of this world.

THE CARNAL CHRISTIAN MUST HAVE THE DESIRE TO LIVE A VICTORIOUS CHRISTIAN LIFE

This is crucial. It does not matter how much the carnal Christian understands what Jesus has done for them, or how much faith they may have to appropriate it for their lives, they have to want to become a spiritual Christian. Paul commanded believers to set their sights on the things above, not the things of this earth:

Since you were brought back to life with Christ, focus on the things that are above, where Christ holds the honored position—the one next to God the Father on the heavenly throne (Colossians 3:1 Gods' Word).

If there is no desire on their part to live their entire life for Jesus, then they will remain a carnal Christian and a person who looks no different from an unbeliever. The choice is up to them.

SUMMARY TO QUESTION 10
WHAT IS THE CARNAL BELIEVER?

Paul called the believers in Corinth "carnal Christians." There were carnal Christians at the time of Paul, and there are carnal Christians that still exist today. While they are believers in Jesus Christ, their life is not one of continually yielding to the Holy Spirit. They are also known as "babies in Christ."

The carnal Christian usually has only a basic understanding of the Bible. Their Christian life is characterized by a lack of spiritual growth. They operate much like an unbeliever. In fact, it is hard to tell the difference between a carnal believer and an unbeliever. They have no real testimony for Jesus Christ in their life.

The good news is that their carnal lifestyle can be overcome. Scripture informs us that these believers do not have to be carnal forever.

First, the person must come to the understanding that Jesus Christ did more than die for the penalty for their sins. He also died so that the power of sin in the life of the believer could be overcome.

Consequently, believers do not have to be slaves of sin any longer. Through the Holy Spirit, we can say "Yes" to God and "No" to sin. This is something which the carnal believer needs to understand.

Second, the carnal Christian must reach out in faith, and accept the help that the Holy Spirit wants to give them to overcome sin. They must believe that God wants them to live a victorious life in Christ. Therefore, by faith, they must yield themselves to the Lord and obey His commandments.

Above all, there must be a willingness, on the part of the carnal Christian, to change their lifestyle. Without a genuine willingness on their part, they will remain as a person who acts just like an unbeliever. The choice to change is entirely theirs.

QUESTION 11

How Can We Control
Our Sinful Desires?

Even after we have believed in Jesus Christ as Savior, Christians still have sinful desires. Each of us is painfully aware of this. The good news is that the Bible tells us that we must control our sinful desires. The following things can help us achieve this goal:

1. WE SHOULD RUN FROM SINFUL SITUATIONS

Sometimes we have to run away from the situation. For example, for the problem of lust, we are told to stay away from situations that tempt us. When Paul wrote to Timothy he instructed him to act in the following way:

> Stay away from lusts which tempt young people. Pursue what has God's approval. Pursue faith, love, and peace together with those who worship the Lord with a pure heart (2 Timothy 2:22 God's Word).

There are certain situations where we must physically leave in order to keep ourselves from sinning. Running away is something we must sometimes do.

2. WE ARE TO PUT TO DEATH OUR OLD NATURE

The Bible commands us to suppress those desires that are sinful. We are to put them to death. Paul emphasized this in his letter to the Colossians:

> Keep your mind on things above, not on worldly things. You have died, and your life is hidden with Christ in God. Christ is your life. When he appears, then you, too, will appear with him in glory. Therefore, put to death whatever is worldly in you: your sexual sin, perversion, passion, lust, and greed (which is the same thing as worshiping wealth) (Colossians 3:2-5 God's Word).

The old nature needs to be constantly put to death. This is something which we must continually work at.

WE MUST KEEP OUR MIND OCCUPIED WITH GODLY THINGS

One way in which to control our sinful desires is to keep our mind occupied with the knowledge of God. Paul wrote about the spiritual weapons available to us through which we can achieve victory:

> With these weapons we break down every proud argument that keeps people from knowing God. With these weapons we conquer their rebellious ideas, and we teach them to obey Christ (2 Corinthians 10:5 NLT).

In a similar manner, Paul told the Philippians to think of good things. In fact, he stressed the necessity of this. He told them:

> And now, dear brothers and sisters, let me say one more thing as I close this letter. Fix your thoughts on what is true and honorable and right. Think about things that are pure and lovely and admirable. Think about things that are excellent and worthy of praise (Philippians 4:8 NLT).

Good things should be occupying our minds.

4. PRAYER HELPS US CONTROL OUR DESIRES

One effective way to control our sinful desires is through the act of prayer. Jesus told us to do the following:

> Stay awake, and pray that you won't be tempted. You want to do what's right, but you're weak (Matthew 26:41 God's Word).

We are to stay awake and pray. In this way, we will be able to resist temptation.

Paul also wrote something similar. He said we are to worry about nothing because we are to pray about everything:

> Never worry about anything. But in every situation let God know what you need in prayers and requests while giving thanks (Philippians 4:6 God's Word).

The Bible emphasizes that prayer will help us control our sinful desires.

5. WE MUST GET RID OF CERTAIN THINGS

We may need to get rid of certain things in our lives that might cause us to sin. Paul wrote to the Romans:

> Let the Lord Jesus Christ be as near to you as the clothes you wear. Then you won't try to satisfy your selfish desires (Romans 13:14 CEV).

If there are things in our lives that are keeping us from becoming more Christ-like, then we should get rid of them. There is no question about this.

6. WE MUST DISCIPLINE OURSELVES

Paul wrote to the Corinthians about the need for self-discipline if we are to win the race in which we are running:

> Everyone who enters an athletic contest goes into strict training. They do it to win a temporary crown, but we do it to win one that will be permanent. So I run—but not without a clear goal ahead of me. So I box—but not as if I were just shadow boxing. Rather, I toughen my body with punches and make it my slave so that I will not be disqualified after I have spread the Good News to others (1 Corinthians 9:25-27 God's Word).

Our bodies need to be under the control of the Lord, not our sinful selves. This takes work, it takes discipline. In the end, victory will be ours.

This sums up how we can control these sinful desires which still plague us. Fortunately, the Lord has provided help for us. It is necessary that we bring these desires under His control.

SUMMARY TO QUESTION 11
HOW CAN WE CONTROL OUR SINFUL DESIRES?

While we who have believed in Jesus Christ have new desires and goals when we become Christians, unfortunately our sinful desires still remain with us. Indeed, as long as we are living in these bodies, we will have to fight these evil thoughts.

Fortunately, there are a number of things that the Bible encourages us to do to keep our sinful desires under control.

To begin with, we should run away from certain situations. This includes the area of the lust, or the strong desire, of our old nature. When confronted with these situations, the best thing we can do is get away from the temptation. Run.

The Bible also says that we are to suppress those parts of our old nature that cause us to sin. The old nature has been defeated by Jesus' work on the cross. It is our responsibility to apply that victory over our sinful desires.

We need to keep our mind occupied on the things which are above. If we think of heavenly things, then we won't be thinking about our sinful wants.

An effective weapon in this fight is prayer. It can help us achieve victory over the desires of the old nature.

Basically, the believer should get rid of all things that cause us to sin. To do all these things takes time and effort. In other words, discipline.

These sinful desires can be controlled—but we must want to do it, and with the help of the Holy Spirit, we can. Indeed, God has given us all of the necessary resources, but the ultimate choice is ours.

How Can We Decide
Right from Wrong?

One of the major questions that each and every human being faces, is how to decide what is right and what is wrong. What standard should be used to determine if a certain act is good or evil? Fortunately, the Christian does not have to be in the dark when it comes to making these types of decisions.

There are a number of points that need to be made about this all-important question.

WE HAVE AN ABSOLUTE STANDARD – THE BIBLE

The world has been given an absolute standard of truth because the living God has revealed Himself to the human race. This is the God of the Bible. His revelation is contained in the Holy Scripture—the Bible. He did not leave us in the dark as to what things are right and what things are wrong.

The Apostle Paul wrote about this divine standard:

> All Scripture is inspired by God and is useful to teach us what is true and to make us realize what is wrong in our lives. It straightens us out and teaches us to do what is right. It is God's way of preparing us in every way, fully equipped for

every good thing God wants us to do (2 Timothy 3:16,17 NLT).

Therefore, we can go to the Scripture to find out what is good and what is evil, what is right and what is wrong.

2. THE STANDARD IS UNCHANGING

Moreover, this standard that has been given by God is unchanging. His Word has been once and for all given. The psalmist wrote:

> Your word, O LORD, is eternal; it stands firm in the heavens (Psalm 119:89 NIV).

His Word stands firm—it has been settled.

Jude wrote about the faith, the body of truth, which has been once and for all delivered to the believers. He put it this way:

> Dear friends, although I was eager to write you about our common salvation, I found it necessary to write and exhort you to contend for the faith that was delivered to the saints once for all (Jude 3 CSB).

We must understand that God has never revised His standard for what is right and what is wrong—it is unchanging.

3. SOMETHING IS ALWAYS RIGHT OR WRONG

Therefore, something that is right, is always right, and something that is wrong, is always wrong. It does not change from generation to generation.

For example, the Bible makes it clear that a believer is not to marry a non-believer:

> Stay away from people who are not followers of the Lord!
> Can someone who is good get along with someone who

is evil? Are light and darkness the same? Is Christ a friend of Satan? Can people who follow the Lord have anything in common with those who don't? (2 Corinthians 6:14,15 CEV).

Believers are only to marry other believers. There are no exceptions to this. Add to this such things as lying, cheating, stealing, and murder. It is always wrong to practice these sins.

THEREFORE, CHRISTIANS CAN ALWAYS KNOW HOW TO BEHAVE

Because God has revealed Himself in these unchanging truths, Christians can always know how to behave. They never have to wonder if certain things are sometimes right, or sometimes wrong. Such things as murder, lying, and stealing, are always wrong. Nobody can ever claim that these are, at times, right. Indeed, they can never be justified as being right.

Therefore, we can make moral decisions with the complete confidence that we are doing the right thing. This is because the God of the Bible has given us His divine standard.

SUMMARY TO QUESTION 12
HOW CAN WE DECIDE RIGHT FROM WRONG?

The living God has revealed Himself to the world through the Bible. In Scripture, the Lord not only tells us who He is, He also tells us how to behave. God has given us a standard of right and wrong. This standard is unchanging from generation to generation.

Therefore, something that is right is always right, and something that is wrong, is always wrong. Indeed, God's standard does not change!

Consequently, the Christian can always know that such things as murder, stealing, and lying are always wrong, while things such as loving others and giving of ourselves to God, are always right.

Therefore, we are able to make moral decisions knowing what is right and what is wrong because of the unchanging standard given to us by the Lord.

What about Questionable Matters That the Bible Does Not Specifically Cover?

When the Bible says that something is right, it is always right. When the Scripture says that something is wrong, then it is always wrong.

However, what are we supposed to do when confronted with something the Bible does not deal with? There are many issues that come up in our daily lives in which the Bible does not have a specific thing to say about. What are we to do?

GOD HAS GIVEN US PRINCIPLES IN HIS WORD

For some people, when specific commands do not exist in Scripture, they use it as an excuse to behave in any way that they please. However, while specific commands may not exist, specific principles do indeed exist. These principles are timeless and they are always relevant. They provide the basis for making difficult decisions. These principles can be applied to all of our moral choices.

They include the following:

IS IT DEALT WITH IN SCRIPTURE?

First, the believer needs to find out whether the particular issue is covered in Scripture. If the matter is covered in the Bible, then there is no question as to what someone should, or should not, do. If the Bible says something is wrong, then it is *always* wrong. There are no exceptions.

Consequently, before we assume that the Bible does not directly deal with the issue in question, we need to search the Scripture to find out if it says anything on the matter. If it does not, then we look at the following principles.

DOES IT ENSLAVE? (IS IT ADDICTIVE)

This question should always be applied to doubtful areas. Does this particular area of conduct cause me to be enslaved? Paul made it clear that he did not want to be enslaved by any habit. He wrote to the Corinthians:

> All things are lawful for me, but all things are not helpful. All things are lawful for me, but I will not be brought under the power of any (1 Corinthians 6:12 NKJV).

We want to have only one master for our life, Jesus. We do not want to be enslaved to anything else.

The Lord Himself has made it clear that we have to choose whom we will serve. In the Sermon on the Mount, He said:

> You cannot be the slave of two masters! You will like one more than the other or be more loyal to one than the other. You cannot serve both God and money (Matthew 6:24 CEV).

The only master that we should have is the Lord. There should be none other.

3. CAN I DO IT IN FAITH?

We also need to ask this question: Is it possible to do this particular thing in faith? The Bible says that whatever is not of faith is sin. Paul said:

But if you do have doubts about what you eat, you are going against your beliefs. And you know that is wrong, because anything you do against your beliefs is sin (Romans 14:23 CEV).

If doubts arise, then it is best to refrain from the activity. We must be able to do it in faith.

4. DOES IT BUILD ME UP AS A CHRISTIAN?

There is a further question which we must answer. Is this behavior something that will contribute to making me a better Christian? Will I grow spiritually stronger by participating in this act? Paul wrote the following:

But I say, walk by the Spirit, and you will not gratify the desires of the flesh. For the desires of the flesh are against the Spirit, and the desires of the Spirit are against the flesh, for these are opposed to each other, to keep you from doing the things you want to do. (Galatians 5:16,17 ESV).

We should only participate in things that will, in some way, further our spiritual growth. If they do not, then we should not do them.

5. DOES IT BUILD UP OTHER CHRISTIANS?

We need to know if this particular act is going to build up other Christians. Paul wrote about the need to practice things that are constructive, or beneficial, not just to us, but also to others. He said to the Corinthians:

All things are lawful, but not all things are helpful. "All things are lawful," but not all things build up. Let no one seek his own good, but the good of his neighbor (1 Corinthians 10:23,24 ESV).

Therefore, our own selfish interests are not the only things that should be considered. We must also think of others.

6. DOES IT HARM OUR BODY?

The Bible says that our body is not our own; it belongs to the Lord. Paul emphasized this when he wrote to the Corinthians:

> Don't you know that you are God's temple and that God's Spirit lives in you? If anyone destroys God's temple, God will destroy him because God's temple is holy. You are that holy temple! (1 Corinthians 3:16,17 God's Word).

Therefore, we should not participate in anything that would cause genuine harm to our body. Ultimately, it does not belong to us.

WOULD JESUS DO SOMETHING LIKE THIS?

Any act that we might do should be considered in light of the behavior of Jesus. "What would Jesus do?" is a fair question to ask. Peter wrote:

> For to this you have been called, because Christ also suffered for you, leaving you an example, so that you might follow in his steps. (1 Peter 2:21 ESV).

Can we actually see Jesus doing this, or some other similar type of behavior? If we cannot, then we should not do it.

WOULD I WANT JESUS TO SEE ME DOING THIS?

There is another question we should answer with respect to Jesus. "Would we want Him to watch us do this thing?" We need to examine the motives for our behavior. "Are we acting as a good representative of Jesus?" Paul wrote:

> And whatever you do, whether in word or deed, do it all in the name of the Lord Jesus, giving thanks to God the Father through him. (Colossians 3:17 NIV).

Another question we should ask is: "Would I want to be engaged in this when Jesus returns?" The Bible says:

> So now, little children, remain in Him, so that when He appears we may have boldness and not be ashamed before Him at His coming (1 John 2:28 CSB).

The idea is to do the things that please Jesus. He is watching.

IS THE CONDUCT FITTING FOR A CHILD OF GOD?

"Is this the sort of behavior that a child of God should become engaged in?" "Does it bring honor or disgrace to Him?"

The Bible warns believers about bringing shame on the name of the Lord. Paul wrote the following to the Romans:

> As Scripture says, "God's name is cursed among the nations because of you" (Romans 2:24 God's Word).

We can bring shame to the name of the Lord.

On the other hand, we are to walk worthy of our calling. Paul wrote to the Colossians:

> Then the way you live will always honor and please the Lord, and you will continually do good, kind things for others. All the while, you will learn to know God better and better (Colossians 1:10 NLT).

Our conduct should be pleasing to the Lord at all times. If it is not, then we should change our conduct.

10. DOES IT PROMOTE EVIL?

We should also ask ourselves if we are promoting evil by our behavior. Scripture says that we are to hate evil. Paul wrote:

> Don't just pretend that you love others. Really love them. Hate what is wrong. Stand on the side of the good (Romans 12:9 NLT)

Christians cannot, in good conscience, support anything that promotes evil. We should never give money, or offer support, to organizations or programs that actively promote sin.

Neither should we personally participate in things that are directly, or indirectly, promoting evil. Believers are not to do anything that would help advance the kingdom of Satan. Nothing whatsoever.

Paul also emphasized that we are to stay away from all things that are evil. He wrote to the Thessalonians:

> Stay away from every form of evil (1 Thessalonians 5:22 CSB).

If the Holy Spirit controls us, then we will not practice anything that promotes evil. Paul wrote to the Romans:

> If your sinful nature controls your mind, there is death. But if the Holy Spirit controls your mind, there is life and peace (Romans 8:6 NLT).

The Holy Spirit leads us into the good. This is where we should always want to be led.

WILL IT CAUSE OTHER BELIEVERS TO STUMBLE IN THEIR FAITH?

Will our conduct be a testimony to the unsaved and an encouragement to believers? Christians are a new creation, and need to act accordingly.

Paul said the following to the Corinthians.:

> Anyone who belongs to Christ is a new person. The past is forgotten, and everything is new (2 Corinthians 5:17 CEV).

In addition, our speech and behavior should not present problems to other believers. Paul wrote to the Romans:

> So don't condemn each other anymore. Decide instead to live in such a way that you will not put an obstacle in another Christian's path (Romans 14:13 NLT).

We should make certain our behavior does not cause others to sin.

THE ISSUE OF FOOD SACRIFICED TO IDOLS

Paul illustrated this point by using the example of food that had been sacrificed to pagan idols. In the city of Corinth, after certain food had been sacrificed on a pagan altar, it was taken to the marketplace and sold. There were some Gentile Christians in the church of Corinth who were buying this food that had been previously offered to idols. The Jewish believers were horrified at this practice. They could not understand why Christians would buy, and then eat, something that had been previously placed as a sacrifice on a pagan altar. They considered such a practice immoral, and were deeply offended that Christians would even consider doing such a thing. Consequently, a division arose between the Jewish and the Gentile believers at Corinth.

Paul responded to the problem in his first letter to the church at Corinth:

> Now about food sacrificed to idols: We know that "We all possess knowledge." But knowledge puffs up while love builds up (1 Corinthians 8:1 NIV).

PAUL MADE THREE IMPORTANT POINTS

He then dealt with the problem by making three points. They are as follows:

THE FOOD WAS NOT CONTAMINATED

First, there was nothing wrong with eating food that had been previously sacrificed to idols. The food was not contaminated in any way. Nothing evil would happen to the Christian who ate the food. Consequently, there is freedom in Christ to eat this food if one so wishes. This is his first point.

THE ACT COULD BE OFFENSIVE TO BELIEVERS

Second, while it was not sinful for Gentile Christians to eat such food, there is another issue that is involved. Is such an act offensive to other believers? This question must be faced. Paul explained the issue in this manner.

> But be careful that this right of yours in no way becomes a stumbling block to the weak (1 Corinthians 8:9 CSB).

We do not want our rights—our freedom in Christ—to become a cause of stumbling for others.

THEREFORE, IT WAS BEST NOT TO EAT OF IT

Third, since eating the food was offensive to other believers, it is best that the Gentile Christians do not continue with this practice. While there is nothing wrong with it, this did cause a problem for other believers. Therefore, for the sake of others, they should refrain from eating food that had been offered to pagan idols.

This principle also applies to us today. While we may be participating in something that is not wrong, in and of itself, this behavior may deeply offend other believers. Therefore, for the sake of the other believers, we will not participate in this behavior.

Paul concluded with the following thoughts:

> So if I hurt one of the Lord's followers by what I eat, I will never eat meat as long as I live (1 Corinthians 8:13 CEV).

Of course, the question arises as to how far we should allow others to influence our behavior. There are some people that will find fault with almost anything that we do. This issue is not black and white. It is one that we may struggle with.

In situations where we are not certain whether our behavior will offend other Christians, we should apply the question that Paul asked. "Can I do this in good faith?" He wrote:

> But if people have doubts about whether they should eat something, they shouldn't eat it. They would be condemned for not acting in faith before God. If you do anything you believe is not right, you are sinning (Romans 14:23 NLT).

We need to be convinced that what we do can be done in faith with a clear conscience. This question should always be addressed.

12. DOES IT GLORIFY GOD?

The overriding principle is this: "Can I do this thing for the glory of God." Paul wrote to the Corinthians:

> So whether you eat or drink or whatever you do, do it all for the glory of God (1 Corinthians 10:31 NIV).

This should be the question we always ask about anything that we intend to do. If we do this, then it will help us decide what to do on these questionable matters.

SUMMARY TO QUESTION 13
WHAT ABOUT QUESTIONABLE MATTERS THAT THE BIBLE DOES NOT SPECIFICALLY COVER?

The Bible is clear on matters that are right and wrong. We are given absolutes in Scripture. Certain things are always right, while other things are always wrong. There are no exceptions to this.

However, there are many issues that face us that Scripture does not specifically cover. When we face these particular matters, we can apply certain timeless principles that the Bible gives us.

The first question we ask is, "Is this dealt with in Scripture?" If not, then we go on to ask a number of other questions. They include: "Does this particular thing enslave?" "Does this type of behavior cause me to be addicted to it?"

We then ask if this can be done in faith. If we have doubts, we should not proceed. Scripture says if we cannot do something in faith, then it is sinful and we should not do it.

We also want to know if it builds us up as a Christian. "Is this practice something that helps make us be more Christ-like?" "Is the behavior something that builds up other Christians?" "Does it make them more Christ-like?"

We should also be certain that this behavior will not harm our body, since it is the temple of the Holy Spirit.

"Can we see Jesus doing something like this?" We should honesty ask, and answer, this particular question when it comes to a doubtful thing.

In addition, "Would I want Jesus to see me doing this?" "Is the conduct fitting for a child of God?" We need to answer these questions.

"Does the act we are contemplating promote evil?" "Will evil be an unintended result from this particular act?"

"Will it cause others to be offended, and to stumble in their faith?" We must be careful that we do not behave in such a way that it will clearly offend others.

The overriding question is, "Does it glorify God?" This is the one question that needs to be answered. If it does, we go forward. If not, then we do not go forward.

We should ask God if our behavior is something that He can truly bless. If it is, then we should go ahead with it.

Whom Is the Believer Supposed to Love?

Once a person becomes a Christian, their life should be characterized by love. Love can be defined as a desire, and a delight, for the highest good for others. It is the desire for *their* best welfare.

LOVE IS THE TEST OF KNOWING GOD

The Bible says that love is the supreme and decisive test of believers. Those who truly know Him, will show it by their love. John wrote:

> Dear friends, let us love one another, for love comes from God. Everyone who loves has been born of God and knows God. Whoever does not love does not know God, because God is love (1 John 4:7,8 NIV).

Those who know the God of the Bible will show His love to others.

IT TELLS US THAT WE HAVE PASSED FROM DEATH UNTO LIFE

Also, when believers love, it demonstrates that they have passed from death unto life. We read the following words from John the Apostle:

> We know that we have passed from death to life, because we love each other. Anyone who does not love remains in death (1 John 3:14 NIV).

This love should be directed in several directions. They include the following:

1. WE ARE TO LOVE GOD

Above all, our love should be directed to God. In the Old Testament this was made clear. In the Law of Moses, we read:

> Hear, O Israel: The Lord our God, the Lord is one. Love the Lord your God with all your heart and with all your soul and with all your strength (Deuteronomy 6:4,5 NIV).

When Jesus was asked about the greatest commandment, He too emphasized that God should be loved above all. Matthew records the following question to Jesus as well as His answer:

> "Teacher, which commandment is the greatest in Moses' Teachings?" Jesus answered him, 'Love the Lord your God with all your heart, with all your soul, and with all your mind' (Matthew 22:36,37 God's Word).

How then do we show that we truly love God? Simple. We keep His commandments. Jesus made this abundantly clear. He said:

> If you love me, you will obey my commandments (John 14:15 NET).

Those who love the Lord will obey His commandments.

2. WE ARE TO LOVE OUR FELLOW BELIEVERS

While Christians are to love everyone, they should have a special love toward the people of God. Indeed, first and foremost, the Christian will be characterized by the love which they show to other fellow believers. Jesus said:

> "I'm giving you a new commandment: Love each other in the same way that I have loved you. Everyone will know that

you are my disciples because of your love for each other"
(John 13:34,35 God's Word).

The mark of the Christian is the love that they show to other believers.
This is the "badge" which all believers should wear.

Peter emphasized the same thing. He wrote:

> Show respect for everyone. Love your Christian brothers and
> sisters. Fear God. Show respect for the king (1 Peter 2:17 NLT).

Again, we find the emphasis on loving fellow believers.

Paul also wrote of the need for Christians to love one another. He
wrote the following to the Thessalonians:

> And may the Lord make you increase and abound in love to
> one another and to all, just as we do to you (1 Thessalonians
> 3:12 NKJV).

Thus, the New Testament repeats this point. Believers must love other
believers.

In another place, the Apostle Paul again emphasized the special love we
are to have for fellow believers:

> Whenever we have the opportunity, we should do good to
> everyone, especially to our Christian brothers and sisters
> (Galatians 6:10 NLT)

Paul personally expressed that type of love to the Corinthians when he
wrote:

> My love *be* with you all in Christ Jesus (1 Corinthians 16:24
> KJV).

One of the ways in which we can show our love to believers, is to help
the ones who are in need. Paul wrote:

When God's children are in need, be the one to help them out.
And get into the habit of inviting guests home for dinner or, if
they need lodging, for the night (Romans 12:13 NLT).

Consequently, Christians show their love to fellow believers in a number of ways.

HUSBANDS ARE TO LOVE THEIR WIVES AND WIVES ARE TO LOVE THEIR HUSBANDS

There is another type of love which believers are to express. Husbands
are to love their wives, and wives are to love their husbands. Paul wrote:

Husbands, love your wives just as Christ loved the church
and gave himself for her (Ephesians 5:25 NET).

We are not only to love our spouses, Paul also emphasized the love we
are to have for our children. He wrote to Titus:

These older women must train the younger women to love
their husbands and their children (Titus 2:4 NLT).

Our children need to be the recipients of our love.

The husband also has the responsibility to take care of their relatives.
Paul wrote to Timothy:

People who don't take care of their relatives, and especially their
own families, have given up their faith. They are worse than someone who doesn't have faith in the Lord (1 Timothy 5:8 CEV).

Husbands are to love their wives and family. This is what the Lord
expects.

4. WE ARE TO LOVE THE UNBELIEVERS

The believer also needs to show love for the unsaved. The Bible says
that God showed His love to the world by sending Jesus:

> For this is the way God loved the world: He gave his one and only Son, so that everyone who believes in him will not perish but have eternal life (John 3:16 NET).

We too are to love those who are lost.

The Apostle Paul spoke of his motivation for ministry—it was the love of Christ:

> For the love of Christ controls us, since we have concluded this, that Christ died for all; therefore all have died (2 Corinthians 5:14 NET).

This could either refer to our love for Christ or the love Christ has for us.

As far as unbelievers are concerned, God does not only provide enough love to fill our hearts and lives, He teaches us to love those whom normally we would not bother with. This concerns those who do not know Christ.

5. WE ARE TO LOVE OUR NEIGHBOR

We are also commanded to love our neighbor. When Jesus was asked about the greatest commandment we find the following response:

> "Teacher, which is the greatest commandment in the Law?" Jesus replied: "'Love the Lord your God with all your heart and with all your soul and with all your mind.' This is the first and greatest commandment. And the second is like it: 'Love your neighbor as yourself.' All the Law and the Prophets hang on these two commandments" (Matthew 22:36-39 NIV).

This is another way of saying "love one another." This would include both believers and non-believers. We are to love humanity because humans, and only humans, have been made in the image of God.

6. WE ARE TO LOVE OUR ENEMIES

Finally, Scripture tells believers to love their enemies. In the Sermon on the Mount, we have these famous words of Jesus:

> But I tell you, love your enemies and pray for those who persecute you (Matthew 5:44 NIV).

This type of love can only come from God. We do not have the capacity to love those who hate us.

This sums up what Scripture says about whom we are supposed to love. It is clear that the Lord wants us to love others.

SUMMARY TO QUESTION 14
WHOM ARE BELIEVERS SUPPOSED TO LOVE?

According to Scripture, there are a number of people that we as believers should love. They include the following:

First, we are to love God. We are to do this with all of our heart. This is primary. First and foremost, we are to love the Lord.

The Bible also says that we are to have a special love for fellow believers. This is the mark of the Christian—our badge. This love may mean helping them with their material needs. Whatever it takes to demonstrate the love of Christ to fellow Christians should be publicly shown.

The Bible says that husbands are to love their wives, and wives are to love their husbands. This is another type of love which the Scriptures command. In addition, parents are commanded to love their children.

Believers are also supposed to love unbelievers. This is how we get the message of Christ to the world. Christ has died for them, and we are commanded to reach them with His good news.

The Bible says that we are to love our neighbor; this includes those who need our help such as the poor. We show the love of Christ by loving our neighbor.

Scripture also says we are to love our enemies. This is not often easy. Indeed, this must be something supernatural.

How Are Believers Supposed to Show Their Love to Others?

The Bible tells us to show our love to others. John wrote the following to believers about how we should love. He put it this way:

> Dear children, let us not love with words or speech but with actions and in truth (1 John 3:18 NIV).

We are to love both in actions, as well as in truth.

The Bible also tells us that our love should come from the heart. Peter wrote:

> Now that you have purified your souls by your obedience to the truth so that you have genuine mutual love, love one another deeply from the heart (1 Peter 1:22 NIV)

The believer is to love from the heart, from our innermost being.

JESUS IS THE AUTHOR OF LOVE

We also find that Jesus Christ is the author of love. It is for His sake that we are to love others. The Bible says:

> We love each other as a result of his loving us first (1 John 4:19 NLT).

We love because of Him.

THERE ARE PRACTICAL WAYS THAT BELIEVERS CAN SHOW LOVE

Scripture gives us a number of practical ways in which we can show love to others. We can sum them up as follows:

1. WE ARE TO LOVE WITHOUT HYPOCRISY

Our love should be done without any hypocrisy. In other words, our love needs to be genuine. The Apostle Paul wrote to the Romans about this necessity. He said:

> Don't just pretend that you love others. Really love them. Hate what is wrong. Stand on the side of the good (Romans 12:9 NLT).

Our love needs to be genuine, to be real. It should not be a "pretend" type of love.

2. WE SHOULD BE PRAYING FOR OUR ENEMIES

One of the ways which we can demonstrate our love for people is by praying for them. This includes our enemies.

Jesus made this clear. In the Sermon on the Mount, we have the following words of our Lord:

> But I say to you, love your enemies, bless those who curse you, do good to those who hate you, and pray for those who spitefully use you and persecute you (Matthew 5:44 NKJV).

Jesus said that we should love our enemies, and pray for those persecute us. This is indeed a practical way in which we can show our love.

3. BELIEVERS SHOULD NOT DO THINGS THAT WOULD HURT OTHERS

True love keeps from doing anything that would injure another person. Paul wrote the following to the church at Rome:

Love does no wrong to anyone, so love satisfies all of God's requirements (Romans 13:10 NLT).

Therefore, we will not do anything that harms our neighbor. Nothing.

WE SHOULD BE SEEKING THE GOOD OF OTHERS

Scripture also tells us that love always seeks the highest good of others. Paul told the Corinthians about this important fact:

No one should seek their own good, but the good of others (1 Corinthians 10:24 NIV).

The interests of others should be our primary concern. Paul emphasized this same truth to the Philippians. He wrote:

Let each of you look out not only for his own interests, but also for the interests of others (Philippians 2:4 NKJV)

We should look out for the good of others. We should not only be looking out for our own interests.

5. WE SHOULD BE CONFRONTING BELIEVERS WHEN THEY SIN

Genuine love from the Lord, lovingly confronts people when they sin. This is first done privately, then before the one or two witnesses, and finally before the church. Jesus gave us this procedure. We read of this in Matthew. It says:

If your brother or sister sins, go and point out their fault, just between the two of you. If they listen to you, you have won them over. But if they will not listen, take one or two others along, so that 'every matter may be established by the testimony of two or three witnesses.' If they still refuse to listen, tell it to the church; and if they refuse to listen even to the church, treat them as you would a pagan or a tax collector (Matthew 18:15-17 NIV).

These are important steps to follow.

The Apostle Paul stated that those who publicly offend others are to be rebuked in the sight of all. Paul wrote to Timothy about this practice:

> But those elders who are sinning you are to reprove before everyone, so that the others may take warning (1 Timothy 5:20 NIV).

There should be confrontation of those who sin. Indeed, they should not be able to get away with it.

THERE SHOULD BE RESTORATION FOR THOSE WHO HAVE SINNED

The goal of confrontation is always restoration. Attempts at restoring people who have sinned should be done in a gentle way. Paul wrote to the Galatians:

> My friends, you are spiritual. So if someone is trapped in sin, you should gently lead that person back to the right path. But watch out, and don't be tempted yourself (Galatians 6:1 CEV).

Those who repent of their sin should be forgiven and accepted back into the local assembly of believers. Paul wrote the following:

> Now it is time to forgive him and comfort him. Otherwise he may become so discouraged that he won't be able to recover. Now show him that you still love him (2 Corinthians 2:7,8 NLT).

The goal is always restoration. It is never punishment for punishments sake.

7. WE SHOULD BE PATIENT WITH ALL

We also show our love by our patience. Scripture says that love is patient toward all. Paul wrote the following to the Thessalonians:

My friends, we beg you to warn anyone who isn't living right.
Encourage anyone who feels left out, help all who are weak,
and be patient with everyone (1 Thessalonians 5:14 CEV).

Patience is to be shown to everyone. In doing so, we reflect the love of
Christ.

BELIEVERS SHOULD AVOID THINGS THAT WOULD CAUSE OTHERS TO STUMBLE

When we love people, we will avoid things that would cause their faith
to stumble. Paul wrote to the Romans:

If you are hurting others by the foods you eat, you are not
guided by love. Don't let your appetite destroy someone
Christ died for (Romans 14:15 CEV).

Our conduct should not be a cause for others to fall.

Paul then reiterated what he had just written:

Don't eat meat or drink wine or do anything else if it might
cause another Christian to stumble (Romans 14:21 NLT).

The believer should not practice things that cause others to stumble.
Instead, we are to do things which spiritually build up others.

BELIEVERS SHOULD TRY TO BE AT PEACE WITH EVERYONE

Another way we can demonstrate the love of Christ is that we should
try to avoid conflict as much as it is possible. Paul wrote to the Romans:

So then, let us aim for harmony in the church and try to
build each other up (Romans 14:19 NLT).

The goal is to be at peace with everyone. Of course, this goal is not
always possible. There are times when people do not want to be peaceable with us.

10. LOVE FORGIVES AND FORGETS

Love forgives and forgets when others sin against us. Paul wrote the following to the believers in Ephesus:

> Be kind and compassionate to one another, forgiving each other, just as in Christ God forgave you (Ephesians 4:32 NIV).

We are to forgive those who have sinned against us, and then move on. In other words, we are not to hold it against them.

LOVE LOOKS AFTER THE NEEDS OF OTHERS

Love also looks after the needs of others. Paul said that our love should be outwardly demonstrated. He wrote to the Corinthians:

> Therefore, before the churches, show them the proof of your love and of our boasting about you (2 Corinthians 8:24 CSB).

Our love can be proven to others.

John also wrote about the necessity of helping others that were in need. He gave a very practical illustration:

> But if anyone has enough money to live well and sees a brother or sister in need and refuses to help—how can God's love be in that person? (1 John 3:17 NLT).

Believers are not to refuse help to other believers who are in need. James wrote the following to the believers:

> If you know someone who doesn't have any clothes or food, you shouldn't just say, "I hope all goes well for you. I hope you will be warm and have plenty to eat." What good is it to say this, unless you do something to help? Faith that doesn't lead us to do good deeds is all alone and dead! (James 2:15-17 CEV).

Genuine love considers the needs of others. This is what Jesus did; this is what we should likewise do.

LOVE SHOWS KINDLY AFFECTION TOWARD OTHERS

Love shows kind affection toward others. Paul wrote to the Romans about expressing genuine affection:

> Love each other with genuine affection, and take delight in honoring each other (Romans 12:10 NLT).

We should attempt to outdo others in demonstrating our love for them. This is another way in which we honor Christ.

13. LOVE CONSISTS OF LAYING DOWN OUR LIVES FOR OTHERS

The ultimate act of love is laying down our lives for someone else. Paul illustrated this in his letter to the Romans. He wrote:

> When we were utterly helpless, Christ came at just the right time and died for us sinners (Romans 5:6 NLT).

This is what Jesus Christ has done on behalf of the believer. We should follow His example.

Thus, from the above, we find many ways in which we can demonstrate our love for others. It is important that we do what the Scripture commands.

SUMMARY TO QUESTION 15
HOW ARE BELIEVERS SUPPOSED TO SHOW THEIR LOVE FOR OTHERS?

The Christian is commanded to love others. Jesus Christ, God the Son, shows us how this can be accomplished. He is the perfect example of what love should be. From Jesus, we learn the following about demonstrating our love toward others:

Jesus was not a hypocrite. Consequently, the Bible says that our love for others should be without hypocrisy. It must be genuine love. We should not fake our love toward anyone.

Love for people can be demonstrated by praying for our enemies. This also follows the example of Jesus. He loved those who hated Him. This type of love takes God's supernatural work in our lives. Often, we want some harm to come to our enemies and we do not want to love them. Yet, God's love tells us to reach out toward our enemies.

True love does not do things that will hurt others. In fact, it only seeks the good of others. Again, we find that Jesus is an example of this. He was always seeking the good of others. So should we.

Love also confronts sinning believers. The loving goal of this confrontation is restoring them to fellowship. If we know someone who has sinned, then we lovingly confront them. Jesus did this, and we should do likewise.

Love shows its patience toward all. In fact, Scripture says the Lord is patient with sinners, waiting for them to turn to Him in repentance. We should also lovingly show patience toward people.

We find that love avoids things that would cause people to stumble. Consequently, we may not want to do certain things for the sake of others. Love puts the needs of others first.

Love desires to live at peace with everyone. While some people may not want to be peaceable toward us, we are commanded to be peaceable toward them.

We should also forgive those who sin against us. In addition, love does not hold a grudge. It both forgives and forgets. Any vengeance against those who sin against us will be done by the Lord. He is the Judge, not us.

Love shows affection toward believers. In fact, Jesus said the mark of the Christian is the love they exhibit one toward another. Thus, no matter what it takes, we should love other believers in Christ.

Finally, those who love will lay down their lives for fellow believers. Jesus, of course, is the greatest example of this. In fact, He laid down His life for His enemies, as well as His friends. We should do no less.

Therefore, as we examine what the Bible says about showing our love toward others, we find, time and time again, that Jesus is our example. Consequently, if we want to behave lovingly, we look to Him for guidance.

QUESTION 16

What Happens When Believers Love Others?

The Bible commands believers to love others. According to Scripture there are a number of things that happen when we love as the Bible commands. They include the following:

1. LOVE COVERS A MULTITUDE OF SINS

The Bible says that love covers a multitude of sins. Peter wrote:

> Most important of all, you must sincerely love each other, because love wipes away many sins (1 Peter 4:8 CEV).

When we reach out to people in love, it can help people forgive some of the sins that we have committed against them, or that they have committed against us. This is one result when we love others.

2. LOVE BUILDS UP

Love also builds people up. Paul wrote:

> In your letter you asked me about food offered to idols. All of us know something about this subject. But knowledge makes us proud of ourselves, while love makes us helpful to others (1 Corinthians 8:1 CEV).

The goal of believers is to build up one another in the faith. We should encourage each other to do good works. The writer to the Hebrews said:

> We should keep on encouraging each other to be thoughtful and to do helpful things (Hebrews 10:24 CEV).

Building up others should be our goal. Love toward others can help accomplish this.

3. LOVE KNITS PEOPLE TOGETHER

Love also knits people together. Paul emphasized this when he wrote to the Colossians. He said the following:

> My goal is that they will be encouraged and knit together by strong ties of love. I want them to have full confidence because they have complete understanding of God's secret plan, which is Christ himself (Colossians 2:2 NLT).

The love of God brings believers in Christ together. This is another example of what our love accomplishes.

4. LOVE GIVES POWER TO PRAYER

Loving our fellow believers gives power to our prayers. John wrote the following to the believers about asking the right things from the Lord, as well as keeping His commandments:

> And whatever we ask we receive from Him, because we keep His commandments and do those things that are pleasing in His sight. And this is His commandment: that we should believe on the name of His Son Jesus Christ and love one another, as He gave us commandment (1 John 3:22,23 NKJV).

Our prayers will be more effective when we love one another.

5. LOVE IS THE OUTCOME OF FAITH

Love is the outcome of faith in Jesus Christ. Paul emphasized this in his letter to the Galatians. He said:

> As far as our relationship to Christ Jesus is concerned, it doesn't matter whether we are circumcised or not. But what matters is a faith that expresses itself through love (Galatians 5:6 God's Word).

Paul said what really counts is faith which is expressed through love.

John said we are to have faith in Christ which will cause us to love one another:

> God wants us to have faith in his Son Jesus Christ and to love each other. This is also what Jesus taught us to do (1 John 3:23 CEV).

Loving one another is a truth which Jesus has taught us. We should follow His example.

SUMMARY TO QUESTION 16
WHAT HAPPENS WHEN BELIEVERS LOVE OTHERS?

The Bible says that showing love to others has a number of practical benefits. Some of them are as follows:

For one thing, the Bible says that love covers a multitude of sins. We can restore a relationship with those whom we have sinned against, or who have sinned against us, by showing our love toward them. By lovingly reaching out to them, there can be a restoration of a broken relationship.

Love also builds people up. It can cause them to be stronger believers in Christ. This is another result of believers loving others.

The love of God also knits believers together in a special way. Indeed, there is something wonderful which happens when believers express their love toward each other.

The Bible also says that love gives power to our prayers. It allows us to be better able to keep the commandments of the Lord, as well as to reach out to others.

Love for one another is the outcome of placing our faith in Jesus Christ. Once we come to Him in faith, we can begin to demonstrate the love of God to believers, and unbelievers alike.

Jesus is our great example in this. As Christians, we should do everything we can to pursue the same course as our Lord. This is a life of love toward others.

Should We
Love Ourselves?

There is a big question as to whether the believer ought to love himself, or herself. Actually, this is not an issue. Every one of us already loves ourselves. The Bible makes this clear. It says:

> No one ever hated his own body. Instead, he feeds and takes care of it, as Christ takes care of the church (Ephesians 5:29 God's Word).

There are a number of important things that we should understand about self-love.

SELF-LOVE IS ONE OF THE SIGNS OF THE END

One of the signs of the end is that people will be lovers of self, rather than lovers of God. Paul wrote to Timothy:

> You should also know this, Timothy, that in the last days there will be very difficult times. For people will love only themselves and their money (2 Timothy 3:1,2 NLT).

When Paul lists a number of sins that will characterize the world at the time of the end, he lists self-love first. In fact, all the other sins in the list flow from this one sin.

If people make themselves, instead of God, the center of their life, then all sorts of problems will proceed from that wrong perspective. The Book of Romans says the following about unbelieving humanity:

> And instead of worshiping the glorious, ever-living God, they worshiped idols made to look like mere people, or birds and animals and snakes (Romans 1:23 NLT).

Instead of worshipping God, humankind worshipped and served themselves. This type of self-love is strongly condemned in Scripture.

WE SHOULD BE CAREFUL OF EXTREMES

We should, however, be careful of going to extremes. Not exercising this sinful type of self-love does not mean punishing our bodies, or denying ourselves of the basic needs of life. We find no such practice with Jesus, or the New Testament church. It is the worship of self, or putting self above everything else, that the Bible condemns.

3. WE ARE SPECIAL TO GOD

The Bible teaches that we are special to God. This is seen in the fact that Jesus Christ, God the Son, came down from heavens glory to die on our behalf. When Paul wrote to the Romans he made the following assessment of Jesus:

> Look at it this way: At the right time, while we were still helpless, Christ died for ungodly people. Finding someone who would die for a godly person is rare. Maybe someone would have the courage to die for a good person. Christ died for us while we were still sinners. This demonstrates God's love for us (Romans 5:6-8 God's Word).

Peter wrote about the great love which the Lord showed toward us through the death of Christ.

In fact, he emphasized the great price Jesus paid for our sins. Jesus' acts showed that we are special to God. He wrote:

> And remember that the heavenly Father to whom you pray has no favorites when he judges. He will judge or reward you according to what you do. So you must live in reverent fear of him during your time as foreigners here on earth. For you know that God paid a ransom to save you from the empty life you inherited from your ancestors. And the ransom he paid was not mere gold or silver. He paid for you with the precious lifeblood of Christ, the sinless, spotless Lamb of God (1 Peter 1:17-19 NLT).

Obviously, we were worth something to God the Father in order for Him to send God the Son, Jesus Christ, to this earth.

Indeed, since the Lamb of God gave His life for us, we are certainly special to Him. We ought to act accordingly. This means, like Jesus, we put others first. We do not put our own selfish interests before anything else.

SUMMARY TO QUESTION 17
SHOULD WE LOVE OURSELVES?

The Bible says that everyone loves themselves. Thus, we do not have to learn how to do this. What we need to learn how to do is to love others. However, the question remains, "Should we love ourselves?"

Scripture says that self-love is one of the signs of the end of the age. People will love themselves more than they will love God. Of course, we see this happening everywhere right now. God is way down on the list of the priorities of most people. At the top of the list, is self.

While this type of self-love is wrong, it is not wrong to be concerned with our own needs. Indeed, we do not find the New Testament characters mistreating their bodies, or hating themselves. What is condemned is the worship of self, not the natural concern we should have for ourselves.

As a matter of fact, we should feel special about ourselves. God the Son, Jesus Christ, left the glory of heaven to come to earth, and died on a cross for our sins. The most precious thing in the universe, the life of God the Son, was given on behalf of the human race. That, in and of itself, makes us special. Indeed, we are special to God.

The key is to have a proper view of ourselves. Not a selfish self-love, but rather a balanced view of who we are. In other words, we need a biblical view of ourselves.

Should the Believer Give Up Their Non-Christian Friends?

Once a person trusts Jesus Christ as their Savior, they become a member of the family of God. This family knows no barriers whether they might be racial, geographical, economical, or social. We are all one in Christ. Male or female, rich or poor, free or slave, we are all in God's family. This is the clear teaching of Scripture. Paul wrote:

> There is no longer Jew or Gentile, slave or free, male or female. For you are all Christians—you are one in Christ Jesus. And now that you belong to Christ, you are the true children of Abraham. You are his heirs, and now all the promises God gave to him belong to you (Galatians 3:28,29 NLT).

However, what do we do with non-Christians? How do we treat them? From Scripture, we can make a few observations.

1. WE ARE TO SEEK THE GODLY

For the Christian, their best friends, and closest acquaintances, should be believers in Jesus. We read in Hebrews:

> We must also consider how to encourage each other to show love and to do good things. We should not stop gathering together with other believers, as some of you are

doing. Instead, we must continue to encourage each other even more as we see the day of the Lord coming (Hebrews 10:24,25 God's Word).

It is important for believers to surround themselves with godly people. This is absolutely essential for us to do.

2. WE ARE TO BE SEPARATE FROM THE SIN OF UNBELIEVERS

The Bible also says that we should separate ourselves from unbelievers—we are not to participate in their sin.

> Therefore "come out from their midst, and be separate," says the Lord, "and touch no unclean thing, and I will welcome you (2 Corinthians 6:17 NET).

We should not participate with unbelievers in their evil deeds. Instead, we are to be separate from their sin.

3. BELIEVERS ARE TO HAVE SOME CONTACT WITH UNBELIEVERS

However, this does not mean that Christians should entirely give up their non-believing friends. There has to be contact with those who do not know Christ. In fact, we find the Apostle Paul going to where the non-Christians were.

We read about this truth numerous times in the Book of Acts. For example, we read the following account:

> So as usual, Paul went there to worship, and on three Sabbaths he spoke to the people. He used the Scriptures to show them that the Messiah had to suffer, but that he would rise from death. Paul also told them that Jesus is the Messiah he was preaching about (Acts 17:2,3 CEV).

We find that the Apostle Paul was accustomed to going to the synagogue, every week, to share his faith with the unbelievers. This is consistent with the command that Jesus gave to His disciples as he was about to ascend into heaven. He commanded:

> And Jesus came and said to them, "All authority in heaven and on earth has been given to me. Go therefore and make disciples of all nations, baptizing them in the name of the Father and of the Son and of the Holy Spirit, teaching them to observe all that I have commanded you. And behold, I am with you always, to the end of the age." (Matthew 28:18-20 ESV).

We are to go into this lost world with the message of Jesus. Therefore, we cannot entirely give up all contact with non-Christians. Yet, we should not make them our closest friends and confidants.

ANOTHER WORD OF ADVICE: OUR BEST FRIENDS SHOULD BE FROM THE SAME SEX

There is one other thing which is necessary to say about friends. Not only should our best friends be believers in Jesus, they should also be of the same sex. In other words, men should have other men as their best friends, and women should do likewise.

Of course, husbands and wives are the exception to this. They should be the best friend of each other. However, apart from this relationship, it is wise to have our closest confidants of the same sex. This will save us from a multitude of problems down the line.

SUMMARY TO QUESTION 18
SHOULD THE BELIEVER GIVE UP THEIR NON-CHRISTIAN FRIENDS?

When it comes to choosing our closest friends, Scripture gives us some very important lessons on what we should do. While not answering this question directly, the principles which the Bible lays down are clear.

The believer should only seek fellow believers as their closest friends. The reason that this is the case, is that we are all members of God's family. These are the people with whom we have spiritual things in common. Since we all belong to the same eternal family, it is fellow Christians who should become our best friends and confidants.

While we are to separate ourselves from unbelievers and we are not to practice their evil deeds, we are not to totally cut ourselves off from them either. They should be the objects of our evangelism as we make known to them the good news about the Lord Jesus. Therefore, we should have some relationship with them but it should not be the most intimate.

In addition, our best Christian friends should be of the same sex. Apart from the husband and wife, who should be the best friend of each other, it is only wise to have members of the same sex as our most intimate friends and confidants. If we do this, then we will save ourselves from a lot of potential grief.

Should a Christian Expect to Be Persecuted?

Persecution is something that has always come along with being a Christian. This should not surprise us. It has been the experience of the godly from the beginning. Scripture tells us the following about the persecution of the righteous:

THE OLD TESTAMENT PROPHETS WERE PERSECUTED

The prophets of the Old Testament were persecuted. The martyr Stephen reminded the people of that when he recounted the history of Israel. He said:

> You stubborn people! You are heathen at heart and deaf to the truth. Must you forever resist the Holy Spirit? But your ancestors did, and so do you! Name one prophet your ancestors didn't persecute! (Act 7:51,52 NLT).

Those who proclaimed God's Word during the Old Testament period were persecuted by others. This is a fact.

2. PERSECUTION IS NOT SOMETHING UNEXPECTED: THEY PERSECUTED JESUS

However, the situation got even worse. Stephen went on to say how they murdered Jesus the promised Messiah. The Book of Acts records him saying the following:

And they killed those who foretold the coming of the Just One, of whom you now have become the betrayers and murderer (Act 7:52 NKJV).

This was the darkest episode in the history of the nation. The Promised One, the Deliverer, was killed by His own people—the people whom He came to save.

3. THE DISCIPLES OF JESUS WERE PERSECUTED

Not only was the Messiah persecuted and killed, we also find that the disciples of Jesus were persecuted. We read the following in the Book of Acts:

Saul agreed with putting him to death. On that day a severe persecution broke out against the church in Jerusalem, and all except the apostles were scattered throughout the land of Judea and Samaria (Acts 8:1 CSB).

Jesus' first disciples were persecuted. The religious leaders wanted to get rid of them as they assumed they had gotten rid of their leader.

4. JESUS SAID THAT WE TOO WILL BE PERSECUTED

Jesus told believers to expect to be persecuted, as He was persecuted. In the last night of His life, our Lord said the following to His disciples:

Remember the word that I said to you: 'A servant is not greater than his master.' If they persecuted me, they will also persecute you. If they kept my word, they will also keep yours (John 15:20 ESV).

As He predicted, His disciples were persecuted.

Jesus also told us to rejoice when others persecute us for the sake of the kingdom. In the Sermon on the Mount, Matthew records Him saying the following:

God blesses you when you are mocked and persecuted and lied about because you are my followers. Be happy about it! Be very glad! For a great reward awaits you in heaven. And remember, the ancient prophets were persecuted, too (Matthew 5:11,12 NLT).

Therefore, persecution is not something that we should think is strange. Indeed, those who follow the Lord should expect it.

WE SHARE IN THE SUFFERINGS AND GLORY OF CHRIST

The symbol of the Christian faith is the cross. Jesus told His followers that they should expect the same sort of treatment that He received. Those who share in Christ's sufferings will also share in His glory. Jesus knows what it means to suffer, so He understands when we suffer.

The Apostle Peter wrote about the persecution that Christians would indeed suffer:

Dear friends, don't be surprised at the fiery trials you are going through, as if something strange were happening to you. Instead, be very glad—for these trials make you partners with Christ in his suffering, so that you will have the wonderful joy of seeing his glory when it is revealed to all the world (1 Peter 4:12,13 NLT).

The believer who shares in the suffering of Christ will also share in His glory. This is what has been promised—this is what will take place.

SUMMARY TO QUESTION 19
SHOULD THE CHRISTIAN EXPECT TO BE PERSECUTED?

The believer in Jesus Christ should not expect everything to be easy all the time. Problems will indeed occur. This includes persecution. We find that all of the Old Testament prophets were persecuted.

In addition, the Promised One, the Messiah, Jesus Christ, was persecuted and murdered. Jesus' own people, the Jewish nation, also persecuted Jesus' own disciples. Therefore, persecution has been the constant theme in Scripture of those who are proclaiming the Lord's message.

In the same manner, for the last two thousand years, those who have believed in Jesus have been persecuted.

However, Scripture tells us to rejoice during these times of persecution. As we share in the sufferings of Christ, we will also share in His glory. This is God's promise to us!

How are Believers to Be Judged?

The New Testament indicates that believers will be judged in three different senses: the judgment of sin, the judgment of self, and the judgment seat of Christ. We can explain them in the following manner:

1. THE JUDGMENT OF SIN

The judgment, of the sin of the believer, occurred on Calvary's cross. Jesus Christ died as a substitute for the sins of the world. Jesus said:

> I assure you, those who listen to my message and believe in God who sent me have eternal life. They will never be condemned for their sins, but they have already passed from death into life (John 5:24 NLT).

Those people, who have believed in Jesus Christ, presently have eternal life. In other words, it is not something merely they will attain in the future, it is something they possess right now.

The Apostle Paul wrote about how Jesus reconciled, or made right, the world to God. This was based on the sacrifice of Jesus Christ. He explained it this way to the believers in the church at Corinth:

> For God was in Christ, reconciling the world to himself, no longer counting people's sins against them. And he gave us this wonderful message of reconciliation. So we are Christ's ambassadors; God is making his appeal through us. We speak for Christ when we plead, "Come back to God!" For God made Christ, who never sinned, to be the offering for our sin, so that we could be made right with God through Christ (2 Corinthians 5:19-21 NLT).

Christ became sin, or a sin offering, on our behalf. The penalty for the sins of the world was placed upon Him.

To the Galatians, Paul emphasized that Christ had been made a curse for us. He wrote the following:

> Consequently, it is clear that no one can ever be right with God by trying to keep the law. For the Scriptures say, "It is through faith that a righteous person has life." How different from this way of faith is the way of law, which says, "If you wish to find life by obeying the law, you must obey all of its commands." But Christ has rescued us from the curse pronounced by the law. When he was hung on the cross, he took upon himself the curse for our wrongdoing. For it is written in the Scriptures, "Cursed is everyone who is hung on a tree" (Galatians 3:11-13 NLT).

Because of His sacrifice on the cross, believers will never have to come into judgment for their sin. Sin has been judged once and for all. This is the great news of the gospel.

2. THE JUDGMENT OF SELF

This is the personal judgment that believers should exercise toward themselves—it has to do with the recognition and confession of sin. This should be a constant practice. John wrote about the need for continual confession:

But if we confess our sins to him, he is faithful and just to forgive us our sins and to cleanse us from all wickedness (1 John 1:9 NLT).

The Apostle Paul spoke of the need for self-examination of believers in Christ. To the Corinthians, he wrote:

Examine yourselves, to see whether you are in the faith. Test yourselves. Or do you not realize this about yourselves, that Jesus Christ is in you?—unless indeed you fail to meet the test! (2 Corinthians 13:5 ESV).

Sins are freely forgiven when confessed. However, unconfessed sin leads to God's disciplining or correcting the believer.

Paul wrote the following to the church in Corinth about the need to discipline those Christians who need correcting:

If someone caused distress, I'm not the one really affected. To some extent—although I don't want to emphasize this too much—it has affected all of you. The majority of you have imposed a severe enough punishment on that person. So now forgive and comfort him. Such distress could overwhelm someone like that if he's not forgiven and comforted (2 Corinthians 2:5-7 God's Word).

This correction is done for the purpose of restoration. However, if we judge ourselves we won't have the need for the church to judge us.

Paul wrote of the necessity of judging, or examining ourselves. He stated it in this manner:

But if we examine ourselves, we will not be examined by God and judged in this way. But when we are judged and disciplined by the Lord, we will not be condemned with the world (1 Corinthians 11:31,32 NLT).

125

It is a good idea that we do this on a regular basis. Indeed, we need to make certain that we are walking the straight and narrow.

The writer to the Hebrews testified that God gives us trials, or testing, for the sake of discipline. He put it this way:

> Endure your discipline. God corrects you as a father corrects his children. All children are disciplined by their fathers (Hebrews 12:7 God's Word).

While testing is certainly not enjoyable, it does help with our personal discipline. In fact, ultimately, it has positive effects although we certainly don't enjoy the process!

3. THE JUDGMENT OF WORKS

There is a third judgment which Scripture speaks about. The Bible says that there will be a judgment of the believer's works at the "Judgment Seat of Christ." This will not be for salvation, but rather for the purpose of rewarding each believer for their faithfulness. Paul wrote about this "reward day" in which the believers will experience:

> For we must all stand before Christ to be judged. We will each receive whatever we deserve for the good or evil we have done in our bodies (2 Corinthians 5:10 NLT).

At that time, believers will be rewarded for their faithful service. Each person will be given rewards based upon their faithfulness. Paul wrote these words to the Corinthians:

> Now, a person who is put in charge as a manager must be faithful (1 Corinthians 4:2 NLT).

The same concept holds true for all believers. Jesus taught this through one of His parables. In His parable, Jesus had the Master saying the following to his servant:

Well done, good and faithful slave! You were faithful over a few things; I will put you in charge of many things. Share your master's joy! (Matthew 25:21 CSB).

Those who are faithful in the little things will be greatly rewarded by God. This is a wonderful promise that we have from the Lord!

In sum, there are three ways in which the believer is judged. In the past, our sins have been judged on the cross; presently, we should be judging, or examining, ourselves; and ultimately, we will be judged, or more properly, rewarded by the Lord.

SUMMARY TO QUESTION 20
HOW ARE BELIEVERS TO BE JUDGED?

The Bible says believers will be judged, but not in the same way as unbelievers. From Scripture, we find that judgment for the believer in Jesus Christ consists of three different aspects. They are as follows:

The New Testament informs believers that our sins were judged on Calvary's cross, when Jesus died as our substitute. The penalty for every sin—past, present, and future—was placed upon Jesus. Since He has paid the penalty for them, we do not have to personally suffer for them ourselves.

This is the message of the gospel—our sins have been taken away! There is a second aspect of judgment. This has to do with the personal judging of ourselves to rid our lives of certain sinful areas. Scripture encourages us to judge, or examine, ourselves.

Finally, there will also be a judgment in the presence of the Lord for those who have trusted Christ as Savior. At that time, believers will be rewarded for their faithfulness to Him.

This judgment day is actually reward day! While our eternal salvation is not earned, our eternal rewards are.

Thus, we should be storing up treasures in heaven as we live this life for Christ, rather than for ourselves.

This briefly sums up the various ways in which believers are to be judged.

What Practical Steps Can We Take Toward Christian Maturity?

As believers, we should desire to live a life which is pleasing to the Lord—to be a mature believer in Christ. There are a number of practical steps that can be taken toward living that mature Christian life. They include the following:

1. BELIEVERS SHOULD COUNT THE COST

First, we must count the cost of following Jesus. There will be a price to pay. Jesus made this very clear. He said:

> For which of you, wanting to build a tower, doesn't first sit down and calculate the cost to see if he has enough to complete it? (Luke 14:28 CSB).

Being a genuine disciple of Jesus involves giving up certain things. Believers do not operate in the same way as those who do not know Christ. There is a price to pay.

WE SHOULD SEVER CONNECTIONS WITH THE PAST

If there are things in the life of the believer that still links them to their sinful past, then, as much as possible, these should be severed from their life. The Bible records what Jesus said about this. Luke records the following:

Then Jesus said to his disciples, "If anyone wants to become my follower, he must deny himself, take up his cross, and follow me" (Matthew 16:24 NET).

There are things in life that must be severed.

3. BELIEVERS SHOULD NOT LOOK BACK

We are to put the past behind, and not look back. Jesus said:

But Jesus said to him, "No one who puts his hand to the plow and looks back is fit for the kingdom of God" (Luke 9:62 CSB).

The believers should always be looking forward. The future is bright!

BELIEVERS SHOULD PUT ASIDE EVERYTHING THAT HINDERS FOLLOWING CHRIST

The believer should put aside everything that keeps them from following Christ. The writer to the Hebrews wrote about laying aside sins that may keep us from serving the Lord. He said:

Such a large crowd of witnesses is all around us! So we must get rid of everything that slows us down, especially the sin that just won't let go. And we must be determined to run the race that is ahead of us. We must keep our eyes on Jesus, who leads us and makes our faith complete. He endured the shame of being nailed to a cross, because he knew that later on he would be glad he did. Now he is seated at the right side of God's throne! (Hebrews 12:1-2 CEV).

In putting everything aside, we are to fix our eyes upon Jesus—He will perfect our faith.

BELIEVERS SHOULD NOT BE SIDETRACKED FROM THE MAIN GOAL

We should keep our eye on the goal and not become sidetracked by unimportant things. The Apostle Paul wrote:

Not that I have already attained this - that is, I have not already been perfected - but I strive to lay hold of that for which Christ Jesus also laid hold of me. Brothers and sisters, I do not consider myself to have attained this. Instead I am single-minded: Forgetting the things that are behind and reaching out for the things that are ahead, with this goal in mind, I strive toward the prize of the upward call of God in Christ Jesus (Philippians 3:12-14 NET).

We are always to keep our eyes on the goal. The prize should always be in our line of sight—always!

BELIEVERS ARE TO BE CONCERNED FOR THE NEEDS OF OTHERS

The believer should also look to the needs of others. Paul wrote about this to the Philippians. He said:

Instead of being motivated by selfish ambition or vanity, each of you should, in humility, be moved to treat one another as more important than yourself. Each of you should be concerned not only about your own interests, but about the interests of others as well. (Philippians 2:3,4 NET).

If the ministry of Jesus could be summed up in one word, the word would be, "others." His life was lived not for Himself but for the benefit of others. The Bible says:

Even as the Son of man came not to be ministered unto, but to minister, and to give his life a ransom for many (Matthew 20:28 KJV).

It is important that we, like Jesus, consider the needs of others.

7. WE SHOULD MAKE CHRIST LORD OF ALL

Above all, Jesus Christ should be Lord of everything in the life of the believer. Paul gave us the overriding principle:

Therefore, whether you eat or drink, or whatever you do, do everything for God's glory (1 Corinthians 10:31 CSB).

Christ should be made Lord of every area of our life.

THE ULTIMATE GOAL IS TO HEAR THESE WORDS FROM THE LORD

The ultimate goal for each believer, when they come face-to-face with the Lord on Judgment Day, is to hear these words from Him:

Well done, good and faithful servant! (Matthew 25:23 KJV).

We should desire to hear these words from Jesus!

Therefore, we need to be faithful to the calling which the Lord has given to us.

SUMMARY TO QUESTION 21
WHAT PRACTICAL STEPS CAN WE TAKE TOWARD CHRISTIAN MATURITY?

When a person wants to truly follow Jesus Christ, then there are certain things to do to reach a mature Christian life.

First, we should count the cost of serving Christ. This is primary. Before we can live a mature Christian existence, we must understand that there will be a cost to pay.

Also, we are to sever any connections with the past that may keep us from maturing spiritually. If there is anyone, or anything, from our past hindering us, then they should be left behind.

In addition, we cannot let anything which we have done in our past hold us back. Our past sins have been forgiven, and forgotten. Indeed, we are to move forward as Christians and not look back.

The Bible also says that we are to put aside those things that presently hinder us. Whatever keeps us from following Him, should be set aside. While this may not be easy to do, it is something which we must do.

Furthermore, Scripture says that we should not allow ourselves to be sidetracked. Indeed, we should always keep our eyes upon the main goal.

Christian maturity will also have us concentrating on the needs of others. This follows the example of Jesus. In fact, if there was to be one word which could sum up the life and ministry of Jesus, it would be "others."

The key is to make Jesus Christ Lord of all. This is what mature Christians do.

If we do follow these steps, then someday we should hear these words from the Lord, "Well done, good and faithful servant."

How Should the LIfestyle of the Christian Be Different from That of the Non-Christian?

Christians should have a different lifestyle than unbelievers. Paul wrote to Timothy to show him how this is accomplished. He said:

> All Scripture is inspired by God and is useful to teach us what is true and to make us realize what is wrong in our lives. It straightens us out and teaches us to do what is right. It is God's way of preparing us in every way, fully equipped for every good thing God wants us to do (2 Timothy 3:16,17 NLT).

We learn a number of things from this verse. They include the following:

CHRISTIANS HAVE THE RIGHT FOUNDATION FOR BELIEF

To begin with, Christians have the correct foundation of knowing the truth—the Scriptures, the Word of the living God. Furthermore, this is divine truth—it is not the mere opinions of humans.

Therefore, whenever we have a question on a subject, we search the divine standard for the answer.

Non-Christians reject the Bible as the only source of divine teaching. They look to other religious writings, their own intellect, or their personal feelings, to decide what they should believe, and how they should act. None of these have any answers. Only the Bible has the answer.

BELIEVERS HAVE A DIVINE STANDARD OF RIGHT AND WRONG

Because we have a divine doctrinal foundation, we can know the difference between right and wrong. The Bible is clear on what we can do, as well as what we cannot do. These issues are not up for discussion.

The unbeliever, on the other hand, has no ultimate source, in which to go, to know how to behave. There is no assurance that their moral choices are correct. Indeed, without the Scripture as an infallible guide, they have no basis whatsoever of calling anything right, or anything wrong.

3. OUR LIFESTYLE CAN BE CORRECTED WHEN WE SIN

Our lifestyle can always be corrected when we go off of the straight and narrow. Scripture tells us that we can acknowledge our sins and then confess them to God. He will forgive us, and then put us back on the right path.

Therefore, we have this guidebook that tells us right from wrong as well as how to get back on the right path. An unbeliever is hopelessly lost in this area. In fact, they do even know what makes something ultimately right and ultimately wrong—let alone how to behave. What a difference there is between them and the believer!

4. WE ARE TO BE INSTRUCTED IN RIGHTEOUSNESS

Finally, the Bible teaches us what is right. It instructs us in the right ways to live. Consequently, we should seek to obey those things that the Lord tells us are righteous.

Unbelievers have no idea what things are righteous, and what things are unrighteous. While they have a conscience that can tell them the difference between what is right and what is wrong, they often do not listen to their conscience.

This sums up some of the ways in which the lifestyle of believers can be different from the lifestyle of the lost.

SUMMARY TO QUESTION 22
HOW SHOULD THE LIFESTYLE OF THE CHRISTIAN BE DIFFERENT FROM THAT OF THE NON-CHRISTIAN?

The Christian should have a different lifestyle than the non-believer. This should be evident in a number of ways.

First, the lifestyle of the believer has its doctrinal foundation in the Bible—the Word of God. Non-Christians reject the Scripture as the only standard of authority on matters of faith and practice. They use their own reasoning powers, or their feelings to determine how they will live. They reject the Bible as the only divine source of truth.

Since the Bible is the final authority on every issue in which it speaks, Christians know the difference between right and wrong. If the Bible says something is wrong, then it is always wrong. Non-believers pay no attention to what the Bible says.

Next comes the issue of sin. The believer will still commit sin. However, we have the divine standard of Scripture to correct us. It tells us that we can confess our sins, and be restored to fellowship with God. The unbeliever has no standard of right and wrong. Therefore, they have nothing from which to correct their sinful ways.

Finally, God has given us an eternal, inerrant guide on how we can live righteously. It tells us the things that we can do to please God. Unbelievers have no idea what it is to please God. In fact, the Scripture makes it clear that they cannot please God apart from believing in Jesus Christ. Left on their own, they have no hope.

This sums up some of the main differences between the non-Christian and their lifestyle, and the Christian and theirs. As can be readily seen, there are huge differences.

When Does God Forgive SIn?

This section looks at how to deal with sin in our lives. We will examine the subjects of sin, confession of sin, repentance, and forgiveness. To live a vibrant Christian life, it is vital that we have an understanding of these important concepts.

QUESTION 23

What Is Sin?

The message of the New Testament is clear: The Bible says that Jesus Christ has come into the world to save us from our sins. Paul wrote to the church at Rome:

> When we were utterly helpless, Christ came at just the right time and died for us sinners (Romans 5:6 NLT).

Christ died for sinners. This is what the good news, or gospel, is all about. But what exactly is sin? What does it mean to be a sinner?

SIN IS DEFINED FOR US

The Bible provides us with a definition of sin. This is found in the first letter from John. He explained sin in this manner:

> Everyone who practices sin also practices lawlessness; indeed, sin is lawlessness (1 John 3:4 NET).

Sin, therefore, is equal to lawlessness. But what precisely is lawlessness? It does not refer to merely the Ten Commandments. Indeed, the Ten Commandments do not cover all cases of sin such as hate, resentment and pride.

Furthermore, the Ten Commandments do not include all the positive commands such as to love one another, to pray without ceasing, and to keep unity among believers. How then, are we to understand lawlessness?

THE LAW IS THE MORAL CHARACTER OF GOD

The Law refers to the moral character of God. This is revealed for us in the hundreds of specific commands and principles for conduct found in the New Testament. Commands are found such as, "Present your bodies as a living sacrifice," "Make no provision for the old nature," and "Bring every thought into captivity." These are all commands of God. When we disobey these commands, we sin, or break the law of God.

THERE IS ONE ALL-INCLUSIVE PRINCIPLE

These commands stem from one, all-inclusive principle that Scripture lays down—we are to do everything for the glory of God. Paul wrote to the Corinthians:

> So whether you eat or drink, or whatever you do, do every-thing for the glory of God (1 Corinthians 10:31 NET).

We are to do all to the glory of God. This means we are to show God off—to make God look good. Again, when we do not do this, then we are sinning.

SIN CAN OCCUR IN FOUR DIFFERENT WAYS

As we examine the issue of sin, we discover that we can sin in one of the four following ways:

1. SIN IS DOING THE WRONG THING

Sin can be defined as doing the wrong thing. When we do something that we are not supposed to do, we sin. Thus, we sin when we do things which are wrong.

2. SIN IS NOT DOING THE RIGHT THING

Sin can also consist of not doing the right thing. If there is something that we know is the right thing to do, yet we do not do it, we are sinning.

3. SIN CAN BE AN OUTWARD ACT

We also discover that sin can be done outwardly. Acts such as lying, stealing, gossiping, or cheating are examples of sinning in an outward manner. It consists of doing things that others can witness.

4. SIN CAN INVOLVE SOMETHING INWARD

However, we do not have to do something outward to be sinning. Sin can consist of evil thoughts, wrong desires, pride, hatred, resentment, or wanting something that does not belong to us. Sinning inwardly is just as wrong as sinning outwardly.

This sums up the four ways in which sin can occur—doing the wrong thing, not doing the right thing, sinning outwardly, and sinning inwardly.

HOW DOES THE BIBLE DESCRIBE SIN?

Sin is a major topic in the Bible. Consequently, the Scripture gives us a number of descriptions of what it means to sin. They are as follows:

1. SIN IS MISSING THE MARK

The God of the Bible has a holy standard of perfection that He has given to us. It is how we are supposed to act and think. When we sin we "miss that mark"—the divine standard that God has set up. Paul wrote:

> For all have sinned, and come short of the glory of God (Romans 3:23 KJV).

All of us have missed that mark—we all have sinned. Furthermore, when something misses a mark, it also hits the wrong thing.

Therefore, this explanation of sin not only has the aspect of missing the proper goal, but also involves hitting the wrong target.

Jesus gave the following standard for believers:

> But I am giving you a new command. You must love each other, just as I have loved you. If you love each other, everyone will know that you are my disciples (John 13:34,35 CEV).

Any feeling other than love toward our fellow believers is sin—it is missing the mark, the standard, which the Lord has set for us.

2. NOT DOING THE RIGHT THING: THE SIN OF OMISSION

Sin can be something we do not do, as well as something that we do. James wrote about sins of omission. He stated it this way:

> If you don't do what you know is right, you have sinned (James 4:17 CEV).

Sins can be of omission as well as of commission. The sin of omission is failing to do what we know is right.

Hence, we are just as guilty if we fail to do something that we are supposed to do, as we are if we do something we are not supposed to do. Each of the actions is sin.

3. SIN IS GOING ASTRAY

Sin is likened in Scripture to us going astray. Isaiah compared it to sheep that wander away from the shepherd:

> All of us were like sheep that had wandered off. We had each gone our own way (Isaiah 53:6 CEV).

This has the idea of walking off the correct path. It is another description of sin.

Jesus talked about the two roads that people can take. In the Sermon on the Mount, He described these roads as follows:

> You can enter God's Kingdom only through the narrow gate. The highway to hell is broad, and its gate is wide for the many who choose the easy way. But the gateway to life is small, and the road is narrow, and only a few ever find it (Matthew 7:13,14 NLT).

When we sin, we stray from the Lord; we walk the wrong path.

4. SIN MEANS BREAKING GOD'S LAW (TRANSGRESSION)

The Bible also calls sin "transgression." This has the idea of breaking the law of God. David, in his prayer of repentance, said:

> Have mercy on me, O God, according to your unfailing love; according to your great compassion blot out my transgressions (Psalm 51:1 NIV)

Sin can be breaking any part of the holy law of God. When we break God's law the Bible says that we "transgress."

5. SIN IS OPPOSING GOD'S WILL (TRESPASS)

Sin is also known as trespass. Basically, a trespass is putting our own will against God's. The Apostle Paul wrote of unbelievers being dead in their own will, or their own trespasses. He put it this way:

> And you were dead in the trespasses and sins (Ephesians 2:1 ESV).

When we place our own desires against those of God, we sin.

This briefly sums up what the Bible calls sin. Since sin is an important topic in Scripture, it is indeed important that we have a thorough understanding of the subject. This will teach us what we should do, as well as what we should not do. In this way, our behavior can please the Lord.

SUMMARY TO QUESTION 23
WHAT IS SIN?

One of the main subjects of Scripture is sin. Sin, in its broadest definition, is any lack of conformity to the perfect character of God, as is revealed in His written Word. It is lawlessness.

However, it is more than breaking the Ten Commandments, since the Ten Commandments do not cover every aspect of sin.

Furthermore, there are many commandments in the New Testament that the believer is instructed to obey. The key principle in all of these commandments, for the believer, is to do everything for the glory of God. When a believer glorifies God, they are not sinning. When we do not glorify God with our behavior, then we are sinning.

Scripture informs us that we can sin in a number of different ways. It can be doing something that we should not do, or not doing something that we should do. In other words, we can commit sins of commission and sins of omission.

Sin can also be something we do outwardly, or it can be a wrong inward feeling. There are a variety of ways in which we can sin.

Sin has been described in various ways. It is illustrated as "missing the mark." This means failing to live up to God's standard.

Sin is also pictured as wandering off the correct path. When we wander off the correct path, then we walk on the wrong path. This is sin.

It is also described as breaking the Law of God—or transgression. We transgress when we break His law.

Sin is also called "trespass." This means opposing God's will with our own.

These descriptions illustrate what it means to sin. It is essential that we understand what sin is, and how to rid sin in our lives. This can only come about from a serious study of the topic.

How Does Sin Affect the Life of the Believer?

The practice ~~of sin is not to be the normal lifestyle of be~~lievers. When we sin, it touches our lives, as well as the lives of others. Indeed, it has a number of effects on us.

1. WE ARE UNABLE TO UNDERSTAND SPIRITUAL TRUTH

For one thing, sin robs us of our ability to understand spiritual truth. The Bible says that it is the Holy Spirit that helps us understand the will of God. Paul wrote the following to the church at Corinth:

> That is what the Scriptures mean when they say, "No eye has seen, no ear has heard, and no mind has imagined what God has prepared for those who love him." But we know these things because God has revealed them to us by his Spirit, and his Spirit searches out everything and shows us even God's deep secrets. No one can know what anyone else is really thinking except that person alone, and no one can know God's thoughts except God's own Spirit. And God has actually given us his Spirit (not the world's spirit) so we can know the wonderful things God has freely given us (1 Corinthians 2:9-12 NLT).

The Christian is completely dependent upon the Holy Spirit if he or she expects to learn anything of permanent spiritual value. We cannot learn these things when we are in sin. Thus, sin in our lives can affect our understanding of spiritual truth.

2. SIN STIFLES THE HOLY SPIRIT'S MINISTRY IN OUR LIVES

Sin quenches the teaching ministry of the Holy Spirit. Paul wrote to the Thessalonians about how our behavior can quench the Spirit, or put out His fire:

> Do not put out the Spirit's fire (1 Thessalonians 5:19 NIV).

We do not want to put out the fire of the Spirit of God. However, we do so when we sin. Indeed, sin keeps the Holy Spirit from working in the ways that He wants to.

Paul explained this in further detail in this section of Thessalonians. For example, sin is not acknowledging the will of God through preaching of the truth of God's Word (1 Thessalonians 5:20); it is not being thankful in everything (1 Thessalonians 5:18); it consists of not praying spontaneously (1 Thessalonians 5:17); it is not rejoicing in whatever circumstances we find ourselves (1 Thessalonians 5:16); and it consists of not keeping away from evil (1 Thessalonians 5:22).

All of these things stifle the Holy Spirit's teaching ministry in our lives. It takes away our ability to understand spiritual truth. Sin does indeed have its consequences.

3. BIBLE STUDY BECOMES UNFRUITFUL BECAUSE OF SIN

Bible study is not a rewarding experience when we sin. The Psalmist wrote about how we should delight in the law of the Lord:

> God blesses those people who refuse evil advice and won't follow sinners or join in sneering at God. Instead, the Law of the Lord makes them happy, and they think about it day and night (Psalm 1:1,2 CEV).

Scoffers reject His law; we should delight in it. However, if we sin, our study of His Word becomes unfruitful.

In fact, Bible study does not accomplish anything. James wrote:

> Obey God's message! Don't fool yourselves by just listening to it. If you hear the message and don't obey it, you are like people who stare at themselves in a mirror and forget what they look like as soon as they leave (James 1:22-24 CEV).

We are supposed to let God's Word act like a mirror to point out areas in our personal life that need changing. Instead, we make excuses, or forget to apply Bible teaching to our everyday situations and decisions. This is what sin can do.

4. SIN ROBS US OF JOY

The Bible says that God wants our joy to be full. John wrote about this to the believers. He put it this way:

> Thus we are writing these things so that our joy may be complete (1 John 1:4 NET).

Our joy should be complete.

We read in Nehemiah how the joy of the Lord should be the strength of the believer:

> He said to them, "Go and eat delicacies and drink sweet drinks and send portions to those for whom nothing is prepared. For this day is holy to our Lord. Do not grieve, for the joy of the LORD is your strength" (Nehemiah 8:10 NET).

Joy is a deep satisfaction that stems from knowing the channel is open between the Lord and us. We are in the place that He approves. It is an inner happiness that is not dependent upon outside circumstances. Sin will rob us of that joy. This is another consequence of sin.

5. SIN TAKES AWAY OUR EXCITEMENT FOR THE THINGS OF GOD

Another problem with sin is that it takes away the excitement of the Christian life. An example of this would be that of King David. After his sin of murder and adultery, he asked the Lord for restoration of his joy:

> Restore to me the joy of your salvation and grant me a willing spirit, to sustain me (Psalm 51:12 NIV).

Sin causes us to lose the joy of our salvation. The Christian may then look to worldly pleasures to fill that void. The empty heart needs to be filled with something. This can lead to further sin. Again, we find that sin has its consequences.

6. SIN ROBS US OF OUR PEACE

Sin also robs us of peace. The believer is to be characterized by an inner calm and contentment. Paul told the Philippians:

> Then, because you belong to Christ Jesus, God will bless you with peace that no one can completely understand. And this peace will control the way you think and feel (Philippians 4:7 CEV).

Paul said that God's peace should rule our hearts:

> Each one of you is part of the body of Christ, and you were chosen to live together in peace. So let the peace that comes from Christ control your thoughts. And be grateful (Colossians 3:15 CEV).

Instead, sin causes anguish of the heart—a complete loss of peace. We read in Psalms:

> When I kept silent, my bones wasted away through my groaning all day long. For day and night your hand was

heavy upon me; my strength was sapped as in the heat of summer (Psalm 32:3,4 NIV).

Our peace with God is lost as a result of sin.

7. SIN HINDERS OUR FELLOWSHIP WITH GOD

Sin robs us of our personal fellowship with God. Indeed, John wrote how sin can cause problems with our relationship with Him:

> What we have seen and heard we announce to you too, so that you may have fellowship with us (and indeed our fellowship is with the Father and with his Son Jesus Christ) (1 John 1:3 NET).

Fellowship can be defined as the consciousness that everything is right between God and us at any moment. The same things that make God happy, will make us happy. Likewise, the things that make God sad, will make us sad. Sin causes problems with that relationship.

8. SIN CAUSES FEELING OF SEPARATION FROM GOD

Sin can cause a feeling of separation between us and the Lord. John wrote the following to the believers:

If we say we have fellowship with him and yet keep on walking in the darkness, we are lying and not practicing the truth (1 John 1:6 NET).

The phrase "we are lying" or "we live a lie," as other translations put it, has the idea of trying to live the Christian life in the energy of the old nature. "Not practicing the truth" refers to those who are ignorant or willfully disobedient of God's commandments.

The believer will experience a lost, or alone, feeling until they get things right with God. These are further consequences of sin.

9. SIN MEANS LOSS OF CONFIDENCE IN PRAYER

Sin also robs us of confidence in our prayer life. John emphasized the lack of confidence which sin can bring. He wrote:

> And by this we will know that we are of the truth and will convince our conscience in his presence, that if our conscience condemns us, that God is greater than our conscience and knows all things. Dear friends, if our conscience does not condemn us, we have confidence in the presence of God, and whatever we ask we receive from him, because we keep his commandments and do the things that are pleasing to him (1 John 3:19-22 NET).

Notice that the final promise is qualified. The Christian must be obedient—they must keep God's commandments to have their prayers answered.

Thus, the Holy Spirit controls only those who ask to be under His control. If we are not under His control at any given moment, then we are sinning.

Scripture says that the Holy Spirit is to direct our prayers. Paul emphasized this to the church at Rome:

> At the same time the Spirit also helps us in our weakness, because we don't know how to pray for what we need. But the Spirit intercedes along with our groans that cannot be expressed in words. The one who searches our hearts knows what the Spirit has in mind. The Spirit intercedes for God's people the way God wants him to (Romans 8:26,27 God's Word).

The Holy Spirit cannot direct our prayers when we are in a state of rebellion against God.

THERE ARE UNANSWERED PRAYERS UNTIL WE CONFESS OUR SINS

Sin can cause our prayers to be unanswered. The psalmist wrote:

If my thoughts had been sinful, he would have refused to hear me.

> But God did listen and answered my prayer (Psalm 66:18,19 CEV).

When a believer commits sin, God does not answer their prayers with a "Yes." God wants to first hear a prayer of confession. It is necessary that we remain obedient to the Lord in order to have our prayer requests granted.

SIN CAUSES THE LOSS OF ANTICIPATION OF CHRIST'S RETURN

Sin also robs us of our anticipation of Christ's return to the earth. Paul said the coming of Jesus Christ is the blessed hope of the believer. He wrote the following to Titus:

> While we look forward to that wonderful event when the glory of our great God and Savior, Jesus Christ, will be revealed (Titus 2:13 NLT).

However, if we are engaged in a certain sin, we are not looking for Christ to return at that moment. In fact, it is probably the last thing that we would want to happen.

12. SIN CAN CAUSE A PERSON TO BECOME FEARFUL OF THE COMING JUDGMENT

Sin will cause us to be fearful of what may be uncovered when Christ judges our works. A Christian should be able to stand before the judgment seat of Christ with confidence.

Paul wrote the following words to the Corinthians about this important truth:

> For we must all appear before the judgment seat of Christ, so that each one may be paid back according to what he has done while in the body, whether good or evil (2 Corinthians 5:10 NET).

The judgment seat can be a time of vindication where all the little things that we have done behind the scenes, that have gone unnoticed by people, will come to light.

John wrote about the confidence we should have when the Lord returns:

> And now, dear children, continue to live in fellowship with Christ so that when he returns, you will be full of courage and not shrink back from him in shame (1 John 2:28 NLT).

Sin will cause us to lose that confidence.

CONFESSION OF SIN IS ABSOLUTELY NECESSARY

Because of what sin can do in the life of the believer, confession of sin is an absolute necessity. The Bible says:

> If we confess our sins, He is faithful and righteous to forgive us our sins and to cleanse us from all unrighteousness (1 John 1:9 CSB).

Confession acknowledges our sin before God. We ask for His forgiveness, and we ask for His help to stop us from doing it again. Confession is absolutely necessary.

CONCLUSION: SIN HAS MANY CONSEQUENCES

In sum, we find that sin has a tremendous effect in the life of the believer. Understanding this should cause us to hate sin and to seek to allow the Holy Spirit to constantly be our guide. It is only then that we can live a life pleasing to the Lord as well as experience God's perfect peace in our hearts.

SUMMARY TO QUESTION 24
HOW DOES SIN AFFECT THE LIFE OF THE BELIEVER?

When we sin, it has consequences for us, as well as for others. Indeed, once we understand the effects of sin, it will motivate us to refrain from sinning. We can give the following illustrations:

The Bible says that sin quenches the ministry of the Holy Spirit in the lives of believers. It can cause Bible study to become unfruitful because we do not feel like hearing from God if we are in sin.

Sin also robs us of joy. It takes away our excitement about the things of the Lord. In fact, the things of the Lord are not given the uppermost importance in our mind if we are sinning.

Sin will hinder our fellowship with God. It can cause a feeling of separation between the Lord and us. This may result in a loss of confidence in prayer.

It may also cause our prayers to be unanswered since we are not allowing the Spirit of God to lead us when we sin.

Sin will cause us to lose our anticipation of the return of Christ. Instead, we are hoping that He will *not* return during the moments we are sinning.

Sin also causes us to become fearful. We realize that we are doing things we should not be doing, and therefore we are afraid.

We lose our spiritual sharpness because of sin. Indeed, sin dulls our spiritual awareness. Indeed, it keeps us from being the type of Christian the Lord desires us to be. Confession is the only remedy that can bring the sharpness back. Once sin has been confessed, we can move forward.

Now that we realize what sin can do to us, it is important that we take the proper steps not to sin.

QUESTION 25

What Is Involved in Confession of Sin?

Once a believer receives Jesus Christ as Savior, they have been forgiven from all of their sins. Indeed, the Bible says our sins are removed from us as far as the east is from the west. This is indeed wonderful news!

Though the believer has been cleansed from their sins once and for all, each of us needs to confess our daily sins to God. This is for the purpose of unbroken fellowship—it is *not* to keep ourselves saved.

Indeed, the blood of Christ that was shed on Calvary's cross settled the believer's guilt once and for all. However, we need to be constantly cleansed from the everyday sins.

We can make the following observations about the importance of confession:

1. A PERSON MUST AGREE WITH GOD

The word "confess" comes from the Greek word *homologeo*. It literally means "to say the same thing." Confession, thus, has the idea of "to agree or to acknowledge fully."

Therefore, when we confess our sins, we say the same thing as God does about our sin. We have God's viewpoint on the matter—we see it as

He does. We also acknowledge with Him that sin has awful disastrous effects.

Confession does not mean rendering lip service, or mouthing deeds with vain repetition. It means calling sin for what it is—sin!

2. WE MUST OWN UP TO THE SIN

We must own up to the fact that the thought, or action, is wrong. We should not try to justify ourselves by rationalizing what we have done— that it really was not sin.

Such rationalizations as "Everyone's doing it" and "It's just a natural human error" or "It's not really so bad" is not real confession. We need to admit that we have sinned. Period.

3. CONFESSION MUST BE SPECIFIC

It is important to name the particular thing to God. We should not be general in our confession. It is the job of the Holy Spirit to reveal specific items of sin in our lives.

John wrote about the importance of walking in the light:

> But if we walk in the light as he himself is in the light, we have fellowship with one another and the blood of Jesus his Son cleanses us from all sin (1 John 1:7 NET).

We are told to examine ourselves—to test ourselves. Paul wrote about the necessity of examining our hearts:

> Examine yourselves to see whether you are still in the Christian faith. Test yourselves! Don't you recognize that you are people in whom Jesus Christ lives? Could it be that you're failing the test? (2 Corinthians 13:5 God's Word).

When we examine ourselves, we are able to determine what needs to be confessed. Thus, we are able to be specific when we confess our sins.

4. CONFESSION SHOULD BE PROMPT

We should not save up our sins until the night, and then confess them. We need to confess them immediately. The Bible says:

> And "don't sin by letting anger gain control over you." Don't let the sun go down while you are still angry (Ephesians 4:26 NLT).

We should not wait to confess our sins. As soon as we realize that we have sinned, we should confess the sin before the Lord.

5. A PERSON SHOULD BE SINCERE ABOUT QUITTING

We must also be sincere about quitting the sin we are confessing. We must have the best intention of not doing it again. This does not mean that we will never commit the sin again—it only means that we are asking God to help us not commit that sin again. This is a crucial element in confession. It will not help if we confess to a particular sin that we are planning to do again!

6. WE REMEMBER THAT JESUS CHRIST IS OUR ADVOCATE – HE IS REPRESENTING US

The Bible says that Jesus Christ is our Advocate. He is the One interceding to God the Father on our behalf. John wrote:

> My little children, I am writing you these things so that you may not sin. But if anyone does sin, we have an advocate with the Father—Jesus Christ the righteous One (1 John 2:1 CSB).

He restores believers to fellowship who sin.

7. AN IDEA OF WHAT TO SAY: A MODEL CONFESSION OF SIN

Our confession of sin to the Lord should go something like this: Lord, I acknowledge that what I have done is wrong. I also agree with you that it is horrible in your sight. With your strength, help me to hate it as much as you hate it. In addition, with the help of the Holy Spirit, I am determined to put this particular sin out of my life, and never do it again.

The key is that we acknowledge our sin before the Lord. We also must ask the Lord's forgiveness, as well as for His help to keep us from doing it again.

This sums up some of the important things we should understand when it comes to confession of sin. It is crucial that we learn what Scripture has to say about confessing our wrongdoings, and then put into practice the things which we have learned.

SUMMARY TO QUESTION 25
WHAT'S INVOLVED IN CONFESSION OF SIN?

While all of our sins are forgiven when we trust Jesus Christ as Savior, there is the issue of the daily sins which we commit. These sins need to be confessed. Thus, for the believer, confession of sin is essential.

Confession can be defined as a sincere admission to God that we have sinned against Him. This confession may be spoken out loud, or it may be spoken of in the heart. It takes only a few words, and can be done at any time, or any place. It is basically agreeing with God that we have sinned against Him.

Confession should be prompt and specific. We should confess our sins to the Lord the moment we commit them—we do not save them up to confess at the end of the day.

There should also be a sincere desire to quit the sin. Confession will not be of any use if we again plan to commit the sin which we have just confessed.

The good news is that we have someone pleading our case to God the Father on our behalf, Jesus Christ. He is the one who represents us before God the Father as our Advocate. He pleads our case so that we can become forgiven.

Why Must We Continually Confess Our Sins?

We are told to continually confess our sins. In First John, we read the following about the necessity of doing this:

> If we confess our sins, He is faithful and righteous to forgive us our sins and to cleanse us from all unrighteousness (1 John 1:9 CSB).

If our sins have been forgiven, once and for all, then why must we continuously confess them? Is there a reason why confession must be something that we continually practice?

The reason is simple: this continuous confession is not to keep ourselves saved, or to be resaved after being lost, it is for the day-to-day relationship we have with God.

ONE CONFESSION DOES NOT LAST FOREVER

We must remember that one confession does not last a lifetime. There is no guarantee from Scripture that the believer is exempt from ever falling into the same sin once it is confessed. Therefore, we must confess our sins each time that we sin.

A NEW TESTAMENT ILLUSTRATION OF THE NEED FOR CONTINUOUS CONFESSION

We have an illustration from the New Testament concerning our need for the daily confession of sins.

When people would go to the public baths, they would wash themselves to the place where they would be clean all over.

However, on the way home, they would gather dirt on their feet. They had to wash themselves again. This time it would not be their entire body, but just their feet that were washed. We find Jesus teaching this to Peter. John records the following:

> Then he poured water into a basin and began to wash the disciples' feet and to wipe them with the towel that was wrapped around him. He came to Simon Peter, who said to him, "Lord, do you wash my feet?" Jesus answered him, "What I am doing you do not understand now, but afterward you will understand." Peter said to him, "You shall never wash my feet." Jesus answered him, "If I do not wash you, you have no share with me." Simon Peter said to him, "Lord, not my feet only but also my hands and my head!" Jesus said to him, "The one who has bathed does not need to wash, except for his feet, but is completely clean. And you are clean, but not every one of you" (John 13:5-10 ESV).

This is the idea behind confession of sin for the believer. The Christian does not have to bathe all over—Jesus Christ forgave all of their sins. Indeed, their sins have been washed away, and they have an eternal standing with God as one of His children. Although we have had our sins washed away, our feet still get dirty—we still commit sin.

THE OLD TESTAMENT IMAGERY OF WASHING

We also find this imagery in the Old Testament. Before a person went to present themselves before God, they went to the altar of sacrifice, and then to the water basin of cleansing—where they would wash themselves. In the Book of Exodus, we read about this. It says:

> Place the altar of burnt offering in front of the entrance to the tabernacle, the Tent of Meeting; place the basin between the Tent of Meeting and the altar and put water in it (Exodus 40:6,7 NIV).

Therefore, we have the need to keep on confessing our day-to-day sins. This is not for the purpose of restoring our salvation—it is for the purpose of restoring fellowship, or our personal relationship, with the Lord. We want to keep that relationship free from anything which might hinder it. This is why we confess our sins.

SUMMARY TO QUESTION 26
WHY MUST WE CONTINUALLY CONFESS OUR SINS?

Although the believer has had their sins forgiven and forgotten, the Bible says that we must continually confess our sins. This confession is not to keep ourselves saved. Rather, it is to keep ourselves in a good relationship with God.

This is illustrated with the public baths which were in use at the time of Christ. Although the person was washed clean in the bath, their feet would become dirty on their way home. Consequently, they had to wash their feet again.

In the same manner, we have been washed clean from all of our sins, yet we still need forgiveness of the daily sins we commit.

The Old Testament presents similar imagery. Before the people could enter the doorway of the tabernacle to offer a sacrifice, they had to wash themselves. This spoke of the daily cleansing that is necessary for those who wish to remain in an intimate relationship with the living God.

Thus, we must understand that one confession does not last forever. Confession must be continual.

What Happens When We Keep Repeating the Same Sin?

One of the practical problems that we face is that we keep repeating the same sin. Many of us confess a particular sin, and then shortly thereafter commit the same sin again. Does this mean our confession was not genuine?

Not necessarily. In cases like this, we need to realize that God, in His grace, has made provision for our repeated failures. We need to make the following observations:

1. THERE MUST BE CONTINUOUS CONFESSION

In 1 John 1:9, the word translated "if" is in, what is known as, a conditional sentence. It can be better translated as "If, and it is probably that you will have to."

Hence, the text assumes that we will have to keep on confessing. The verb "confess" is in the continuous tense in Greek which denotes continued, repeated action. It can be literally translated, "Keep on confessing as a habit of life."

God has provided this remedy because He is aware of our human weaknesses. In other words, as long as we live in these sinful bodies, we will need to confess our sins.

2. CONFESSION LOOKS BACK TO WHAT WE HAVE DONE

Confession looks backward to what we have already done. It takes care of past sins which we have already committed. It is primarily curative of something that has happened.

It does not, in and of itself, give power for us to overcome temptation the next time it occurs. Thus, we should expect to return to the Lord in the future to confess other sins.

3. THE CONSCIENCE MAY BE HARDENED IF WE DO NOT CONFESS

Once a person does a certain sin a number of times, the conscience becomes hardened. The particular sin becomes easier and easier to commit. When a person gets to the place to where they are enslaved to a particular sin, they need to face the issue and ask for God's help.

4. THE GOOD NEWS: WE DO NOT HAVE TO KEEP ON SINNING

The good news is that we do not have to be slaves to sin. Paul gave the following illustration of this when he wrote to the Romans. He said:

> Well then, should we keep on sinning so that God can show us more and more kindness and forgiveness? Of course not! Since we have died to sin, how can we continue to live in it? Or have you forgotten that when we became Christians and were baptized to become one with Christ Jesus, we died with him? For we died and were buried with Christ by baptism. And just as Christ was raised from the dead by the glorious power of the Father, now we also may live new lives. Since we have been united with him in his death, we will also be raised as he was. Our old sinful selves were crucified with Christ so that sin might lose its power in our lives. We are no longer slaves to sin. For when we died with Christ we were set free from the power of sin. And since we died with Christ, we know we will also share his new life (Romans 6:1-8 NLT).

Sin does not have to have any more authority over the believer. The Bible says that we are dead to sin, but alive to God.

Therefore, sin does not have to rule our lives any longer. Jesus Christ died so that we would not have to experience the penalty of sin. His death also allows the believer not to experience the power of sin. As Paul wrote, believers need no longer be slaves to sin—we have been freed from its authority.

Consequently, we do not have to keep on repeating the same sin. This is a message that the Lord wants all believers to hear and understand.

SUMMARY TO QUESTION 27
WHAT HAPPENS WHEN WE KEEP REPEATING THE SAME SIN?

There are times when believers repeat the same sin over and over again. God has told us what we must do in these cases.

When we continue to repeat a sin, we must also continue to confess that sin. Though confession does not give us the power to overcome a particular sin, it does remind us that the act we are confessing is sinful.

If we persist in a certain sin for a long period of time, it is likely that our conscience will become hardened. If this happens, we must ask the Lord to help us change our behavior. It does not do us any good if we are in denial over this.

The good news is that we do not have to keep on sinning. The death of Jesus Christ on the cross of Calvary has freed us from the power of sin. No longer do believers have to be slaves to sin. We now belong to Jesus—He is our Master. Sin, therefore, has no more authority over us.

This is an important truth which we need to understand, as well as put into practice.

How Does Sin Affect Our Relationship with Others?

The Bible says that sin not only has an effect upon us, but it also affects our relationship with other people. The Bible is explicit in the way sin affects believers. We can list a number of these things in the following manner:

1. There Is a Lack of Compassion for Others

This first point is of extreme importance. The sincere concern that believers have for unbelievers, is affected by sin in our life. When we are in sin, thoughts of unbelievers, and their need to turn to Christ for forgiveness, do not arise. Those who are trapped in sin are indifferent to the plight of the lost.

Contrast this to the attitude of the Lord Jesus. The Bible says that when He viewed the multitudes, He had compassion on them. Matthew records His response:

> When he saw the crowds, he had compassion on them because they were bewildered and helpless (Matthew 9:36 NET).

We want to have the same compassion as Jesus. However, if we are practicing some particular sin, we will not have that compassion.

2. WE BECOME INTERESTED IN THE WRONG THINGS

If we are in the midst of sin, we tend to be interested in everything except that which is of utmost importance.

When Paul addressed the Colossians, he emphasized the things that Christians should be interested in. He put it this way:

> Therefore, if you have been raised with Christ, keep seeking the things above, where Christ is, seated at the right hand of God (Colossians 3:1 NET).

If we are in sin, then our mind will not be on heavenly things. Consequently, opportunities to testify to our faith in Christ are bypassed.

3. WE MAKE NO IMPACT FOR CHRIST

There is another result of being in sin. We do not leave the proper impact on those people whom we meet. We fail to see, that those whom God brings us into contact with, are people who need to know Christ. Our zeal to testify to Jesus Christ has been lost. Sin has robbed us of an opportunity to glorify God.

Paul wrote to the Corinthians about the one principle which should guide all of our behavior—the ultimate glory of God:

> Therefore, whether you eat or drink, or whatever you do, do all to the glory of God (1 Corinthians 10:31 NKJV).

Sin stops us from keeping this important commandment. When we are in sin, we are not thinking of God's glory at that moment.

In sum, we find that sin has some very practical consequences—consequences which none of us want to experience!

SUMMARY TO QUESTION 28
HOW DOES SIN AFFECT OUR RELATIONSHIP WITH OTHERS?

Sin not only has its effects on the believer, it also affects our relationship with others. This occurs in a number of ways. They include the following:

First, it can cause a lack of compassion for others—especially for the lost. When we are in sin, we lose all concern for those who do not know Christ. In fact, we are only thinking of ourselves.

Second, sin makes our interests something other than the interests of the Lord. Our minds are certainly not on the things of God if we are in sin.

Finally, it can cause a loss of opportunity of making an impact for Christ. These opportunities will continue to be missed as long as we are practicing certain sins.

Sin keeps us from following this particular commandment: that we should do all to the glory of God.

Thus, sin has a number of undesired effects. This gives us further reasons as to why we should refrain from sinning against the Lord.

QUESTION 29

What Is Temptation?

The Greek word translated "temptation" in the New Testament has a number of meanings.

Temptation can be defined as "testing." It can have the idea of testing metal to determine if it is genuine.

It is also used in the sense of luring one to commit sin. Thus, the exact meaning of the term is determined by the context.

There are a number of things that the Bible says about temptation or testing. They are as follows:

1. WE SHOULD ASK GOD TO HELP US FROM YIELDING TO TEMPTATION

We are told to pray to escape the temptation that may lead us to sin. In the Sermon on the Mount, Jesus told His disciples that they should pray in the following way:

> And don't let us yield to temptation, but deliver us from the
> evil one (Matthew 6:13 NLT).

We should ask the Lord to help us when we are tempted. Indeed, we need His help.

2. TEMPTATION IS NOT SIN

It is important to realize that it is not a sin to be tempted—all of us are tempted. Jesus Himself was tempted by the devil. We read the following in Matthew:

> Then was Jesus led up of the Spirit into the wilderness to be tempted of the devil (Matthew 4:1 KJV).

Jesus was tempted—but He did not give in to the temptation. Therefore, we should not feel guilty when we are tempted. Being tempted to sin is not the same as giving in to sin.

3. THERE ARE PURPOSES FOR OUR TEMPTATIONS OR TESTINGS

Temptation, or testing, always has a purpose. God tests us to bring out the best in us. In other words, we are tested to make us better people.

On the other hand, Satan tempts us to bring out the worst in us. Being tested, or tempted, is not sin—it depends upon what we do with the temptation. It can bring out the best in us, or the worst in us.

AN ILLUSTRATION OF TEMPTATION

The following illustration may help. Let us say, for example, that as you walk along your street you find a wallet. You look at the wallet and discover that it contains a large sum of money, in cash. There is also a driver's license and credit cards identifying the owner of the wallet. This constitutes a temptation.

One could attempt to justify taking the money by saying the owner does not need it, since he has numerous credit cards and obviously is financially well off.

What is done with the temptation determines whether the believer does, or does not, sin. If you return the wallet to the owner, then you have not sinned. If you keep the money for yourself, then it is a sin.

The testing, or temptation, is not sin. However, how you respond to the test determines whether or not you have sinned.

4. WE SHOULD EXPECT TO EXPERIENCE TESTING

Temptation, or testing, is something that the believer should expect to experience. Jesus said the following to His disciples:

> I have told you these things so that in me you may have peace. In the world you have trouble and suffering, but have courage—I have conquered the world" (John 16:33 NET).

Therefore, we should not be surprised when we are tested. In fact, we should expect to be tempted. Therefore, we should always be ready to deal with the temptations which come our way.

Jesus also said:

> If you had anything in common with the world, the world would love you as one of its own. But you don't have anything in common with the world. I chose you from the world, and that's why the world hates you. Remember what I told you: 'A servant isn't greater than his master.' If they persecuted me, they will also persecute you. If they did what I said, they will also do what you say (John 15:19-20 God's Word).

Trusting Christ as Savior does not relieve the believer from temptation. On the contrary, there will usually be more things put in the Christian's path in order to cause us to fail. Again, we should not think it strange when these trials cross our path.

The Apostle Peter wrote:

> Beloved, do not be surprised at the fiery trial when it comes upon you to test you, as though something strange were happening to you (1 Peter 4:12 ESV).

Temptation will always come to the believer in this life. This is something that we must realize—we will always face testing or temptation.

5. WHEN TEMPTED, WE SHOULD NOT DOUBT THE LORD'S GOODNESS

The enemy often uses temptation to cause us to doubt the Lord's goodness. We are given the idea that God wants to stop our fun. It seems that the only things that we really enjoy, are those things which are sinful. This idea attempts to place a wedge between God and us. If we think that God does not always have our best interest in mind, then we will doubt His goodness. We must understand this as we deal with the various testings, or temptations, which come our way.

6. SOME TEMPTATIONS ARE DESIGNED FOR OUR WEAKNESSES

This point is extremely important. The believer needs to understand that temptations have been especially made to fit our own particular weakness. There would be no sense in tempting someone in an area where there was no weakness.

Whatever our particular weakness may be, it is in that area in which we will be tempted. It is therefore important that we understand our own weaknesses, and honestly admit that we need to be strengthened in these areas.

If we understand the areas in which we are vulnerable, then we can be on guard for temptations in that area. It is crucial that we take such precautions.

7. TEMPTATIONS ARE OFTEN CLEVERLY DISGUISED

Often the temptations are cleverly disguised. They are not so obviously evil. Sometimes they do not really seem that bad. This can fool us into thinking that the particular deed is not wrong—or at least not that wrong.

However, this type of temptation can have just as devastating of an effect as something that is obviously wrong.

The Bible says that Satan disguises himself as an angel of light. Paul wrote:

> And no wonder, for even Satan disguises himself as an angel of light (2 Corinthians 11:14 NET)

Therefore, we should not be surprised when we are tempted in a clever way.

This provides us with some of the important truths regarding temptation, or testing. It is essential that we always keep them in mind.

SUMMARY TO QUESTION 29
WHAT IS TEMPTATION?

Temptation, or testing, is something that the Bible says the believer will experience. It is not a sin to be tempted. Temptation, or testing, is neutral.

God's purpose is to bring out the best in us, while the enemy tries to bring out the worst. Therefore, it all depends upon what we do with the temptation, or testing, which we are given. If we do not give in to the temptation, then we have not sinned.

All of us will continue to experience temptation as long as we are in this body. Until we meet the Lord, this is something which we will always have to put up with.

We should not doubt the goodness of the Lord when we are tempted. He allows these testings to make us into stronger Christians.

We also need to be aware of the fact that many temptations are cleverly disguised. They may not seem like temptations when we first encounter them. Thus, we always need to be on guard.

Knowing these things should help us in our constant battle against temptation.

QUESTION 30

How Should a Person Resist Temptation?

What should we do when temptation comes to us? There are times that we do not feel that we can resist certain temptations. What are we to do when these occasions arise?

The Bible has a number of things to say on the subject.

WE CAN OVERCOME TEMPTATION

The Scripture promises that we will not be placed in a situation that we are not able to handle. Paul wrote about this to the Corinthians:

> No trial has overtaken you that is not faced by others. And God is faithful: he will not let you be tried too much, but with the trial will also provide a way through it so that you may be able to endure (1 Corinthians 10:13 NET).

We are not tempted beyond what we can bear. God promises there will always be a way of escape. We need to claim that promise.

THE WAYS IN WHICH TO ESCAPE TEMPTATION

There are various ways in which believers can escape the temptation to sin. They include the following:

WE SHOULD NOT PUT OURSELVES IN A TEMPTING SITUATION

Sometimes the answer to resisting temptation is as simple as not getting ourselves in the situation. If we know we have a certain weakness with a particular sin, then it is important that we avoid situations where we could be tempted with that sin.

2. WE SHOULD RUN FROM TEMPTATION

If we do find ourselves in a situation where we are being tempted, then the correct response is to leave immediately. The Bible says:

> Flee also youthful lusts; but pursue righteousness, faith, love, peace with those who call on the Lord out of a pure heart (2 Timothy 2:22 NKJV).

The best thing to do is to run from temptation.

3. WE SHOULD BE FILLED WITH THE SPIRIT

Being filled, or controlled, by the Holy Spirit is the best way to deal with temptation. Paul wrote the following to the Ephesians:

> Don't get drunk on wine, which leads to wild living. Instead, be filled with the Spirit (Ephesians 5:18 God's Word).

It is vital that we should be filled with the Spirit. This has the idea of the Spirit controlling our behavior.

4. WE SHOULD KNOW THE SCRIPTURE

Believers can resist temptation by citing Scripture. When Jesus was tempted by the devil, He responded by quoting Scripture. Three times Jesus said, "It is written." We read about this in Matthew:

> Jesus answered, "It is written: 'Man does not live on bread alone, but on every word that comes from the mouth of God." Then the devil took him to the holy city and had him

stand on the highest point of the temple. "If you are the Son of God," he said, "throw yourself down. For it is written: 'He will command his angels concerning you, and they will lift you up in their hands, so that you will not strike your foot against a stone.'" Jesus answered him, "It is also written: 'Do not put the Lord your God to the test.'" Again, the devil took him to a very high mountain and showed him all the kingdoms of the world and their splendor. "All this I will give you," he said, "if you will bow down and worship me." Jesus said to him, "Away from me, Satan! For it is written: 'Worship the Lord your God, and serve him only'" (Matthew 4:4-10 NIV).

This is a good example for how we should deal with temptation when it comes our way. We fight the temptation by quoting Scripture.

THE BIBLE SAYS THE FOLLOWING IN THE BOOK OF PSALMS:

How can a young person maintain a pure lifestyle? By following your instructions! With all my heart I seek you. Do not allow me to stray from your commands! In my heart I store up your words, so I might not sin against you (Psalm 119:9-11 NET).

Believers need to read, study, and memorize the Bible. Time should be set aside each day for doing this. Paul wrote:

Let Christ's word with all its wisdom and richness live in you. Use psalms, hymns, and spiritual songs to teach and instruct yourselves about God's kindness. Sing to God in your hearts (Colossians 3:16 God's Word).

We should take the time to study and know God's Word. In this way, we will be able to fight the temptations which come our way.

5. WE NEED TO ASK THE LORD IN PRAYER FOR HELP

Prayer is another part of overcoming temptation. We should ask the Lord for His help. The writer to the Hebrews said:

> So we can go confidently to the throne of God's kindness to receive mercy and find kindness, which will help us at the right time. (Hebrews 4:16 God's Word).

We must ask for God's help if we want to resist the temptation. He has promised to help us if we ask Him. Therefore, it is important that we ask.

6. WE MUST REALIZE THAT JESUS CHRIST UNDERSTANDS OUR PROBLEMS

The Bible says that Jesus knows exactly what we are going through. He suffered similar temptations to us when He was upon the earth. The Bible says the following of Him:

> Therefore, it was necessary for Jesus to be in every respect like us, his brothers and sisters, so that he could be our merciful and faithful High Priest before God. He then could offer a sacrifice that would take away the sins of the people. Since he himself has gone through suffering and temptation, he is able to help us when we are being tempted (Hebrews 2:17,18 NLT).

Jesus recognizes our needs. Thus, we can talk to Him about them when we pray. He has been there; He understands.

7. WE MUST STARVE THE OLD NATURE

One of the practical things we can do to escape temptation is to starve the old nature. Paul wrote the following command to the Colossians:

> Therefore, put to death whatever is worldly in you: your sexual sin, perversion, passion, lust, and greed (which is the

same thing as worshiping wealth). It is because of these sins that God's anger comes on those who refuse to obey him. You used to live that kind of sinful life. Also get rid of your anger, hot tempers, hatred, cursing, obscene language, and all similar sins. Don't lie to each other. You've gotten rid of the person you used to be and the life you used to live (Colossians 3:5-9 God's Word).

It is important that we do what we can to keep the old nature from being active in our lives. We do not need to feed it, but rather to starve it.

8. WE MUST FEED THE NEW NATURE

If we feed our new nature, then that will help us overcome temptation. We need to be occupied with the things of Christ to help overcome temptation. Paul emphasized this when he wrote to the Colossians. He said:

In its place you have clothed yourselves with a brand-new nature that is continually being renewed as you learn more and more about Christ, who created this new nature within you. In this new life, it doesn't matter if you are a Jew or a Gentile, circumcised or uncircumcised, barbaric, uncivilized, slave, or free. Christ is all that matters, and he lives in all of us. Since God chose you to be the holy people whom he loves, you must clothe yourselves with tenderhearted mercy, kindness, humility, gentleness, and patience. You must make allowance for each other's faults and forgive the person who offends you. Remember, the Lord forgave you, so you must forgive others. And the most important piece of clothing you must wear is love. Love is what binds us all together in perfect harmony (Colossians 3:10-14 NLT).

The new nature must be fed. This fact is stressed in Scripture.

9. BELIEVERS MUST TAKE CARE OF THEIR BODY

As much as is possible, we ought to exercise our physical bodies. Paul wrote to Timothy about this. He said:

> Physical exercise has some value, but spiritual exercise is much more important, for it promises a reward in both this life and the next (1 Timothy 4:8 NLT).

There is profit in bodily exercise. Since the body is the temple of the Holy Spirit, believers should do their best to maintain good physical health. However, in doing this, it must always be acknowledged that the spiritual part is what is most important. Yet, the body should not be neglected—it is not evil.

10. WE MUST UNDERSTAND THAT DELIVERANCE IS NOT A ONCE AND FOR ALL EXPERIENCE

If a person does not yield to a certain temptation, this does not mean they will never be tempted again, or that the next time they will be strong enough to resist. Temptation is something that continually happens to us. Consequently, we must continue to trust in God to help us overcome temptations.

The temptations of Jesus by the devil continued throughout His ministry. After the forty-day temptation was over the Bible says:

> So when the devil had completed every temptation, he departed from him until a more opportune time (Luke 4:13 NET).

The devil came back and tempted Jesus, and he will come back to tempt us. We must recognize this truth.

11. TEMPTATION HAS BEEN DEFEATED

Believers need to realize that Jesus Christ has overcome all temptation. John wrote about this important truth:

Dear children, you belong to God. So you have won the victory over these people, because the one who is in you is greater than the one who is in the world. These people belong to the world (1 John 4:4 God's Word).

Although Jesus was tempted, He did not sin. This means that the believer does not have to sin either. When we sin, it is because of our own choice—it is not because we have to sin. This is certainly good news!

In sum, if we want to resist temptation, then the Bible gives us a number of ways as to how we can accomplish this. The key is to know how to resist, and then follow through with what we know to be true.

SUMMARY TO QUESTION 30
HOW SHOULD A PERSON RESIST TEMPTATION?

As long as Christians are in this sinful world, they will be tempted to sin. This is a fact.

Consequently, it is important that we know how to resist the temptation. Since the Bible provides the solution to the various temptations we face, it is our responsibility to put these solutions into practice. The Bible says that temptation can be overcome. The following things should be helpful:

First, do not put yourself in a situation where there is temptation. Many problems can be overcome if we simply do not allow ourselves in certain situations. Indeed, there will be no temptation whatsoever.

When temptation occurs, run from it! This is the biblical command. We should not try to stay and fight it. That is a certain way to lose.

The key is being filled, or controlled, by the Holy Spirit. If we allow Him to guide us, then we can resist the testings, or temptations, which come our way.

It is important to know the Scripture when facing temptation. Jesus resisted temptation by quoting Scripture. He is our example. We should certainly do the same.

Believers need to ask the Lord for help when being confronted with temptation. The Lord has promised to help us. Prayer, therefore, is an important weapon in the battle against temptation.

There is something else. We need to realize that Jesus Christ understands what is taking place when temptation occurs. He was tempted in all points, the Bible says. Yet Scripture also emphasizes that He never sinned. This means that we do not have to give in to the temptation. The Lord always provides a way of escape.

The Bible talks about starving the old nature, and feeding the new nature. The old nature is what urges us to sin. We should not do anything to encourage it. On the other hand, the new nature always urges us to seek after the Lord. This is why we are commanded to feed the new, and starve the old.

It is also necessary to take care of our physical bodies. Contrary to what some have taught in the past, they are important.

Although we may defeat temptation, we need to realize that it will occur again. It is a constant battle. The good news is that Jesus Christ has defeated temptation, and that we can also. However, we must always remember how we are to go about doing it.

What Lessons Can be Learned From Jesus' Temptations?

The Bible says that after His baptism Jesus was tempted by the devil. We read the following in the Gospel of Matthew:

> Then was Jesus led up of the Spirit into the wilderness to be tempted of the devil (Matthew 4:1 KJV).

This temptation of Jesus is recorded in three of the four gospels: Matthew, Mark, and Luke.

LESSONS LEARNED FROM JESUS' TEMPTATION

There are a number of lessons that can be learned from Jesus' temptation by the devil. They include the following:

1. EACH CHRISTIAN WILL BE TEMPTED

Like Jesus, the Christian will be both tested, and tempted. The question is not "if," but "when." We will be tempted to sin. Jesus' life serves as a pattern for ours. If the Lord was tempted, then we will be tempted. We can all count upon this.

2. THE TEMPTER COMES AT VULNERABLE MOMENTS

The tempter came to Jesus at His most vulnerable moment—when He was tired and hungry. Matthew wrote:

> After he fasted forty days and forty nights he was famished. The tempter came and said to him, "If you are the Son of God, command these stones to become bread." (Matthew 4:2,3 NET).

We should expect the same. When we are at our weakest, we should expect the tempter to come. This is how he works.

3. THROUGH JESUS WE CAN OVERCOME TEMPTATION

As humankind's representative, Jesus, the last Adam, was obedient in His response to temptation.

On the other hand, the first Adam, also representing humankind, miserably failed. Therefore, through Jesus we can succeed when tempted. However, if we allow the old Adamic nature to prevail, we will fail. Paul wrote:

> There isn't any temptation that you have experienced which is unusual for humans. God, who faithfully keeps his promises, will not allow you to be tempted beyond your power to resist. But when you are tempted, he will also give you the ability to endure the temptation as your way of escape (1 Corinthians 10:13 God's Word).

It is possible to overcome temptation through trusting Jesus. This is a promise of Scripture. He will always provide a solution to our temptations.

4. WE SHOULD APPEAL TO SCRIPTURE WHEN TEMPTED

Jesus resisted the devil by appealing to Scripture three times in succession. For example, when tempted, Matthew records Jesus saying the following:

> Jesus responded, "The Scriptures also say, 'Do not test the Lord your God'" (Matthew 4:7 NLT).

We should do the same as our Lord. Therefore, the importance of knowing God's Word cannot be overemphasized.

5. JESUS UNDERSTANDS WHAT WE ARE EXPERIENCING

Scripture says we have a High Priest, who has Himself been tempted in all ways, who is able to help us when we are tempted. The writer to the Hebrews said:

> Therefore since we have a great high priest who has passed through the heavens, Jesus the Son of God, let us hold fast to our confession. For we do not have a high priest incapable of sympathizing with our weaknesses, but one who has been tempted in every way just as we are, yet without sin. Therefore let us confidently approach the throne of grace to receive mercy and find grace whenever we need help (Hebrews 4:14-16 NET).

Jesus understands what we are going through. He was tempted just as we are tempted. Therefore, when we talk to Him about our temptations, we are talking to someone who understands.

6. WE SHOULD GO ABOUT GETTING THE RIGHT THINGS IN THE RIGHT WAY

There is another valuable lesson we learn from Jesus' temptations. What Jesus was offered by Satan—the rulership of this world—is something that He has now earned through His sinless life, and His death on Calvary's cross. This reiterates an important biblical lesson—we should not go about trying to get the right things in the wrong way. The right things will come to us in the right time.

These are some of the important things which we learn as we examine the temptations which Jesus received. We need to put these lessons into practice.

SUMMARY TO QUESTION 31
WHAT LESSONS CAN BE LEARNED FROM JESUS' TEMPTATIONS?

The Bible says that Jesus Christ was tempted by the devil for some forty days. We learn a number of lessons from the temptation of Jesus.

First, we will be tempted—there are no exceptions. If our Lord was tempted, then we, as His servants, will also be tempted.

Second, we will be tempted when we are the most vulnerable. The tempter came to Jesus after He had fasted for forty days. He was certainly in a weakened state. In the same way, the tempter will approach us when we too are in a weakened state.

Third, we can achieve success through trusting in Jesus. He overcame temptation—we can too. He has promised to see us through any temptations we may experience.

Fourth, like Jesus, we should appeal to Scripture when we are tempted. Indeed, we find that each time Satan tempted Jesus, the temptations were answered with quotations from Scripture. God's Word is our powerful ally when we are being tempted.

Fifth, because He experienced temptation, Jesus understands our temptations. He has been through them, and He has overcome them. Consequently, when we talk to Him about the testings we are experiencing, we are speaking to someone who understands.

Finally, with Jesus as our example, we should go about getting the right things in the right way. Instead of receiving immediate gratification, Jesus resisted the easy way. Rather than bowing down to Satan, so that he could receive the promised kingdom, Jesus refused the offer. The kingdom, which was rightfully His, needed to come by way of the cross. Jesus had to die. Thus, He did not take the easy way out.

In the same manner, we need to get the right things in the right way, and at the right time. This is another lesson we learn from His testings.

Therefore, as we examine what Jesus went through in His encounter with the devil, there are a number of valuable things we can learn. We need to learn them, as well as to put them into practice.

Does A Person Have
to Keep On Sinning?

Sometimes, when believers continue to commit sin, they assume that they cannot help themselves. They see themselves as slaves to sin. Yet the Bible teaches that we do not have to keep on sinning. Paul wrote to the Romans:

> Well then, should we keep on sinning so that God can show us more and more kindness and forgiveness? Of course not! Since we have died to sin, how can we continue to live in it? (Romans 6:1,2 NLT).

The message in this is clear—we do not have to keep on sinning.

WE ARE NO LONGER SLAVES TO SIN

Jesus Christ has saved believers to live a victorious life in Him. His death not only freed us from the penalty of sin, it has also freed us from the power of sin. The Bible teaches that before we trusted Christ, we were slaves to sin.

Previously we had no choice but to obey our sinful desires. Once we have been born again, we have a new nature that is able to keep from sinning. We have been set free! The Bible says:

> For whatever is born of God overcomes the world. And this
> is the victory that has overcome the world—our faith (1
> John 5:4 NKJV).

Through Christ Jesus we have overcome the world. We have been set free!

Jesus Himself said:

> Therefore if the Son makes you free, you shall be free indeed
> (John 8:36 NKJV).

Therefore, the Son has set us free from sin. This is what Jesus clearly taught.

We also read that Jesus came to give abundant life to all those who believe. John records Him saying the following:

> The thief comes only to steal and kill and destroy; I have
> come so that they may have life, and may have it abundantly
> (John 10:10 NET).

Consequently, because of the death of Jesus Christ on the cross of Calvary, believers no longer need to be under the bondage of sin. We can live life abundantly.

AN ILLUSTRATION OF GOING BACK TO THE OLD BOSS

Let us illustrate what it means to be under the bondage of sin. Suppose a person used to work at a warehouse, and let us suppose they visit this place where they have not worked for some thirty years.

As they walk in the door they see their old boss. Upon seeing this person, the old boss shouts, "I'm glad you're finally here, get to work." The boss gives the former employee all these orders to fill, and then tells them to sweep up the place when they have finished filling the orders. The person then immediately takes off their good clothes, and puts on some older clothes, and begins to do all that the old boss commanded.

What would you say if someone did something like that? You would say, "The person is acting foolish. Why are they still obeying the old boss? They are not under his authority any longer!"

Yes, it would be silly for a person to obey a boss that has not had authority over them for some thirty years. Yet, believers are just as unwise when we allow ourselves to sin. Our old nature does not have authority over us any longer. When we succumb to it, we are obeying a boss who does not control us. This is not a wise thing to do.

THERE ARE THREE REASONS WHY CHRISTIANS KEEP ON SINNING

When a Christian is still in the bondage of a particular sin, it is usually for one of the following three reasons. They can be summed up in this manner:

1. WE DO NOT UNDERSTAND THAT CHRIST HAS WON THE VICTORY

Many Christians do not understand that Jesus Christ not only took away the penalty for our sins, He also took away the power that sin has over us. His death has freed us from the power of sin. Paul wrote:

> Our old sinful selves were crucified with Christ so that sin might lose its power in our lives. We are no longer slaves to sin. For when we died with Christ we were set free from the power of sin (Romans 6:6,7 NLT).

Therefore, it is important that Christians realize they do not have to be in bondage to sin any longer. Jesus has taken care of this.

2. WE DO NOT HAVE ENOUGH FAITH THAT SIN CAN BE OVERCOME

There are other believers who do understand that the death of Christ was to save us from the power of sin, yet they do not have enough faith to believe that it can happen to them.

While Christ can free others from the bondage of sin, these people, for some reason, do not believe that Christ can free them. They lack the faith that it can happen in *their* life. Until they reach out to God in faith and trust Him to take care of their sin, they will remain in bondage. The key is to believe that they, too, can be set free.

What is needed is not great faith, but rather a small amount of faith in the greatness of God. Jesus said to His disciples:

> "You didn't have enough faith," Jesus told them. "I assure you, even if you had faith as small as a mustard seed you could say to this mountain, 'Move from here to there,' and it would move. Nothing would be impossible" (Matthew 17:20 NLT).

Scripture stresses that the object of our faith is what is important. Therefore, the person in this position needs to reach out to the Lord with only the amount of faith they have. God will do the rest.

3. WE DO NOT WANT TO OVERCOME A PARTICULAR SIN

This final group of people may indeed understand that Christ has removed the power of sin from their lives. Also, they may have sufficient faith to trust Him to keep them from sinning. Their problem is that they do not *want* to stop doing a particular sin. They may be enjoying committing a particular sin, and do not want it to stop.

Others may want to continually be punished for their own sin—even though Christ has taken their punishment. Whatever the case may be, those in this category are not allowing the Lord to deal with their personal sin. Paul wrote:

> Therefore do not let sin reign in your mortal body so that you obey its desires (Romans 6:12 NET).

In this case, the person needs to let the Holy Spirit change their behavior. They need to see their sin as God sees it—something horrible.

Whatever the reason they continue sinning, God has something better for them—if they give it up.

This sums up why some believers in Christ continue to keep on sinning, even though they do not have to.

SUMMARY TO QUESTION 32
DOES A PERSON HAVE TO KEEP ON SINNING?

The answer to this question is a clear "No." Once we have trusted Christ as Savior, we no longer need to serve sin. This is what the Scripture clearly teaches. When we sin, we are the only ones to blame—it is our fault, and no one else can be blamed. The good news is that Christ has overcome sin so that we too can be overcomers by faith. Therefore, the believer does not have to keep sinning, or be a slave to sin.

When believers continue to sin, there is usually one of three reasons as to why this is occurring. They can be simply stated as follows:

Some people do not understand that Christ has saved us from the power of sin, as well as from the penalty of sin. Therefore, we do not have to be under the bondage of sin any longer. In other words, they have not comprehended the wonderful biblical truth that we can be free from the authority of sin. Consequently, they continue in sin.

Others may understand what Christ has done for them, but they lack the faith to trust Him to free them from personal sins. They need to realize that Christ can free them, as He has freed others from the bondage of sin. They are capable of rejecting sin.

A final group simply does not want to stop doing a particular sin, or sins. They want to remain slaves to some evil behavior. Until they truly ask the Lord to change their attitude, He cannot bless them as He desires.

This explains why some Bible-believers think they have to keep on sinning. However, they do not. The Lord has indeed set us free.

QUESTION 33

Will Anyone Get to the Place Where They Are Without Sin? (Perfectionism)

Is it possible to get to the place where we are without sin? There are some people who not only believe that it is possible, but they believe that they have achieved it! This is known as sinless perfection, or perfectionism.

THERE IS NO SINLESS PERFECTION IN THIS LIFE FOR ANYONE

While some people may believe that they have reached a state of sinless perfection, the Bible is very clear on this issue. It is not possible for a person to be absolutely without sin in this life. The Apostle John wrote:

> If we say, "We aren't sinful" we are deceiving ourselves, and the truth is not in us. God is faithful and reliable. If we confess our sins, he forgives them and cleanses us from everything we've done wrong. If we say, "We have never sinned," we turn God into a liar and his Word is not in us (1 John 1:8-10 God's Word).

This letter, written to believers, makes it plain that we will never reach a sinless state in this life. We are only fooling ourselves if we think that we have somehow become sinless.

THE TESTIMONY OF PAUL

The Apostle Paul acknowledged that he had not reached a sinless state. Indeed, when he wrote to the Philippians he penned the following words:

> It's not that I've already reached the goal or have already completed the course. But I run to win that which Jesus Christ has already won for me. Brothers and sisters, I can't consider myself a winner yet. This is what I do: I don't look back, I lengthen my stride, and I run straight toward the goal to win the prize that God's heavenly call offers in Christ Jesus (Philippians 3:12-14 God's Word).

He realized that he had not attained any place of perfectionism, and that he never would in this life. We should realize the same thing.

SOMEDAY WE WILL BE LIKE HIM

There will, however, be a time in the future when we are without sin. This will occur when we see Jesus face-to-face:

> Beloved, now we are children of God; and it has not yet been revealed what we shall be, but we know that when He is revealed, we shall be like Him, for we shall see Him as He is (1 John 3:2 NKJV).

We look forward to the time when we will see Him face-to-face. However, until that time, we will remain in this body and we also will remain sinners. This is the teaching of Scripture.

SUMMARY TO QUESTION 33
WILL ANYONE GET TO THE PLACE WHERE THEY ARE WITHOUT SIN? (PERFECTIONISM)

It is clear that all of us are born with a sinful nature. Even after we believe in Jesus Christ, our sin nature still exists. Indeed, there is a constant struggle between the two natures for control of our behavior. Thus, believers are in a battle—the flesh, or the old nature, against the Spirit.

This battle will continue until the Lord returns. Thus, no Christian should consider his or herself as having "arrived." There is always new territory to conquer. Sinless perfection is not possible in this life. There will always be room for improvement. Anyone who thinks differently is only fooling themselves.

What is Repentance?

One of the most important truths that we can understand is the doctrine of repentance. In fact, we learn that the doctrine of repentance is one of the basics of the Christian faith. The writer to the Hebrews stated:

> So let us stop going over the basics of Christianity again and again. Let us go on instead and become mature in our understanding. Surely we don't need to start all over again with the importance of turning away from evil deeds and placing our faith in God (Hebrews 6:1 NLT)

The teaching about repentance is primary to the faith. Consequently, it must be one in which we take time to study.

TWO DIFFERENT WORDS IN THE NEW TESTAMENT ARE TRANSLATED "REPENT"

There are two different Greek verbs translated "repent" in the New Testament. One word means "a regret of past actions." It has the idea of being sorry for something that was done.

The other word translated "repent" means "a complete change of attitude." When the Bible encourages the believer "to repent," what is being encouraged is this latter use of the Greek word "repent."

Therefore, when we speak of "repentance"—the act of repenting—we are not speaking of being sorry for what we have done, or merely having a change of mind about our sins. We are speaking of an entire change of attitude—it is an entire new view of who we are.

REPENTANCE BRINGS A NEW ATTITUDE

Thus, repentance is a complete shift of attitude toward God and our sins. The Bible commands people to repent. We find this in the ministry of John the Baptist:

> In those days John the Baptist came into the wilderness of Judea proclaiming, "Repent, for the kingdom of heaven is near" (Matthew 3:1,2 NET).

The people needed to change their ways since the coming kingdom was at hand.

Jesus told people they had to repent. Luke records Him saying:

> No, I tell you; but unless you repent, you will all likewise perish (Luke 13:3 ESV).

Repentance is defined as turning from sin and turning to God. In the Book of Acts we read the following:

> I have declared to both Jews and Greeks that they must turn to God in repentance and have faith in our Lord Jesus (Acts 20:21 NIV).

A new attitude is brought about when people repent.

IT IS NOT REFORMATION OR SORROW

Repentance is not reforming our life, nor is it penance, or an attempt to atone for sins. Repentance is change—it is more than sorrow. Godly sorrow is what leads to repentance.

The Apostle Paul wrote to the church of Corinth:

> For even if I made you sad by my letter, I do not regret having written it (even though I did regret it, for I see that my letter made you sad, though only for a short time). Now I rejoice, not because you were made sad, but because you were made sad to the point of repentance. For you were made sad as God intended, so that you were not harmed in any way by us. For sadness as intended by God produces a repentance that leads to salvation, leaving no regret, but worldly sadness brings about death. For see what this very thing, this sadness as God intended, has produced in you: what eagerness, what defense of yourselves, what indignation, what alarm, what longing, what deep concern, what punishment! In everything you have proved yourselves to be innocent in this matter (2 Corinthians 7:8-11 NET).

True repentance is not reformation, or sorrow. It is an actual change of direction.

JESUS SPOKE OF TRUE REPENTANCE

True repentance is shown by the example of one of the sons in a story told by Jesus. Matthew records Jesus giving the following illustration:

> What do you think? A man had two sons. And he went to the first and said, 'Son, go and work in the vineyard today.' And he answered, 'I will not,' but afterward he changed his mind and went. (Matthew 21:28,29 ESV).

True repentance will be followed by actions—not merely feeling sorry for something that has been done.

TRUE REPENTANCE REGRETS THE WAY WE HAVE ACTED IN THE PAST

When we genuinely repent, it will cause us to regret the way in which we have acted in the past. Paul wrote the following to the church at Rome:

And what was the result? It was not good, since now you are ashamed of the things you used to do, things that end in eternal doom (Romans 6:21 NLT).

True repentance brings about regret.

REPENTANCE SEES OURSELVES AS WE REALLY ARE

When a person repents, they have a new view of who they are. We find a number of examples of this in Scripture.

Peter saw himself in a different light after Jesus performed the miracle of the fish. We read about this in the Gospel of Luke:

But when Simon Peter saw it, he fell down at Jesus' knees, saying, "Depart from me, for I am a sinful man, O Lord" (Luke 5:8 ESV).

Peter recognized his sinfulness in the presence of Jesus.

Isaiah was a prophet of God. However, when he was confronted with the holiness of God, he realized his true nature:

"Woe to me!" I cried. "I am ruined! For I am a man of unclean lips, and I live among a people of unclean lips, and my eyes have seen the King, the LORD Almighty" (Isaiah 6:5 NIV)

Isaiah saw himself for whom he truly was in the presence of God.

Job protested his innocence and righteousness while he was going through his suffering. However, this changed when he came face-to-face with God:

My ears had heard of you but now my eyes have seen you. Therefore I despise myself and repent in dust and ashes (Job 42:5,6 NIV).

If we judge ourselves by human standards, then we may regard ourselves as decent, moral people. However, once we compare ourselves to the living God, then we have an entirely differently view of who we are. When the Holy Spirit reveals our sin, and how it looks before a holy God, we begin to realize the awfulness of sin. This understanding of sin is what causes a change of behavior—repentance.

THE CRIMINAL NEXT TO JESUS ON THE CROSS REPENTED

We find another example of true repentance with the criminal who was next to Jesus on the cross. He changed his attitude toward Jesus, as well as to the other criminal who was crucified.

At first, he joined with the other criminal in taunting Jesus. However, this soon changed. We read the following in Luke:

> One of the criminals hanging beside him scoffed, "So you're the Messiah, are you? Prove it by saving yourself—and us, too, while you're at it!" But the other criminal protested, "Don't you fear God even when you are dying? We deserve to die for our evil deeds, but this man hasn't done anything wrong." Then he said, "Jesus, remember me when you come into your Kingdom." And Jesus replied, "I assure you, today you will be with me in paradise" (Luke 23:39-43 NLT).

This criminal realized that the one being crucified next to him was the Messiah. Therefore, he had a change of heart. He asked Jesus if he too could be part of God's kingdom. Jesus promised the criminal that he would enter paradise with Him.

REPENTANCE MAY NOT MANIFEST ITSELF IN EMOTION

Often, we equate repentance to some emotion of sorrow, or remorse. While emotion may accompany repentance, it is not the same thing. Repentance is not showing emotion for our past deeds—it is changing the way we act in the present. It is possible for a person to truly repent of their past actions, and show little, or no, emotion. The key is not the emotion that is shown—the key is the change in behavior. Those who truly repent have determined that their life must change.

GOD IS THE ONE WHO GIVES PEOPLE THE OPPORTUNITY TO REPENT

God is the One who grants people the opportunity to repent. We read in the Book of Acts:

> When they heard these things they became silent; and they glorified God, saying, "Then God has also granted to the Gentiles repentance to life" (Acts 11:18 NKJV).

The possibility of repentance is His gracious gift to us.

Paul wrote to Timothy about this very thing. He said that God may allow, or grant, certain people to repent—if we act patiently toward them:

> And the Lord's servant must not be quarrelsome but kind to everyone, able to teach, patiently enduring evil, correcting his opponents with gentleness. God may perhaps grant them repentance leading to a knowledge of the truth (2 Timothy 2:24,25 ESV).

We also read in the Book of Acts:

> God exalted him at his right hand as Leader and Savior, to give repentance to Israel and forgiveness of sins (Acts 5:31 ESV).

God moved on the hearts of people, by means of the Holy Spirit, to cause them to repent. Again, He is the One who brings about this repentance.

PETER AND JUDAS ARE EXAMPLES OF TRUE AND FALSE REPENTANCE

The difference between true repentance, and mere sorrow for sin, can be seen in the examples of Peter and Judas.

When Peter realized he betrayed Jesus, he was sorry for his sins. Matthew records the episode as follows:

> After a little while the men standing there approached Peter and said, "It's obvious you're also one of them. Your accent gives you away!" Then Peter began to curse and swear with an oath, "I don't know the man!" Just then a rooster crowed. Peter remembered what Jesus had said: "Before a rooster crows, you will say three times that you don't know me." Then Peter went outside and cried bitterly (Matthew 26:73-75 God's Word).

Peter went outside and cried intensely. He realized what he had done. Indeed, there was genuine sorrow for his act.

Judas, on the other hand, instead of coming to God in repentance, decided to take his own life. We read of his fate in Matthew. He explained it in this manner:

> So Judas threw the money into the temple and left. Then he went away and hanged himself (Matthew 27:5 NIV).

He did not repent—he only had remorse for what he had done. There is a huge difference between the two.

THE RESULTS OF GENUINE AND NON-GENUINE REPENTANCE

Peter was restored to fellowship after his repentance. In addition, he was given the honor of preaching the first sermon for the church on the day of Pentecost.

In that sermon, Peter urged the people to do the same thing that he had done, repent:

> Peter replied, "Each of you must turn from your sins and turn to God, and be baptized in the name of Jesus Christ for the forgiveness of your sins. Then you will receive the gift of the Holy Spirit" (Acts 2:38 NLT).

Peter received the forgiveness of the Lord. He learned that repentance can restore us into a right relationship with the Lord.

We note the fate of Judas, the betrayer. Judas, according to Scripture, went to his appointed place of judgment. This is explained in the Book of Acts:

> Judas bought a field with the money he received for his treachery, and falling there, he burst open, spilling out his intestines. The news of his death spread rapidly among all the people of Jerusalem, and they gave the place the Aramaic name Akeldama, which means "Field of Blood" (Acts 1:18,19 NLT).

When Jesus came back from the dead, on Easter Sunday morning, Peter was found with the rest of the disciples. He did not leave the company of believers—he did not kill himself. He repented of what he had done, and had returned to be with the other believers.

Judas, on the other hand, only felt remorse. Instead of repenting, and looking to godly people for support, he hanged himself.

These two men provide examples of what we should do, and should not do, when we sin. With Peter, we should repent. We do not merely feel sorry for what we have done.

Instead, we own up to our sin, and have a determination to change our behavior. The Lord will then restore us to fellowship. This is what genuine repentance is all about.

SUMMARY TO QUESTION 34
WHAT IS REPENTANCE?

The Bible commands believers to repent from their sins. The word repentance means an entire change of attitude toward sin. It is not merely feeling sorry that you did something, or having a change of mind about it. True repentance is turning from sin and turning to God.

We find that the doctrine of repentance is one of the basic doctrines of the Christian faith.

In Scripture, we have an example of true repentance in the case of Simon Peter—the man who denied knowing Christ. After he denied Jesus, Peter realized that he had committed a terrible sin.

Thus, he repented. He was restored to the ministry, and was given the honor of preaching the first sermon for the church on the Day of Pentecost. This is an example of genuine repentance.

There is also an example of sorrow without repentance in the case of the traitor, Judas. Judas had betrayed Jesus for money. When he realized his sin, he hanged himself instead of coming to God in true repentance. His repentance was not a turning to God—only the action of feeling sorry for what he had done.

Consequently, we learn the lesson that we must not merely feel sorry for what we have done. True repentance means turning to God, determining to change our behavior, and asking for His forgiveness.

How Can We Overcome Habitual Sin?

Unfortunately, with some believers, there are certain sins that are habitual. It usually consists of one or two certain sins that a person feels enslaved to. How can we deal with this type of sin, and escape the bondage it brings? What can someone do?

BELIEVERS CAN BE OVERCOMERS

The Bible provides help in these matters. Indeed, Jesus' death and resurrection gives us power to be overcomers with respect to sin. His death was not only from the penalty of sin, it also saved us from the power of sin. Sin, therefore, does not have to master us.

The Bible commands us not to let sin rule over us:

> Therefore do not let sin reign in your mortal body so that you obey its desires (Romans 6:12 NET).

Sin does not have to rule over us.

TEMPTATION CAN BE OVERCOME

The bad news is that we will be tempted with sin; the good news is that we can overcome sin. The Bible makes this clear. Paul wrote the following to the Corinthians:

No trial has overtaken you that is not faced by others. And God is faithful: he will not let you be tried too much, but with the trial will also provide a way through it so that you may be able to endure (1 Corinthians 10:13 NET)

We can overcome temptation—we do not have to fail.

HOW CAN WE OVERCOME HABITUAL SIN?

This being the case, there are several things we can do to deal with habitual sin. They include the following:

1. WE SHOULD KNOW OUR ENEMIES

First, we should know who our enemies are—the world, the flesh, and the devil. We must have an understanding of who is attempting to defeat us.

The world system is attempting to make each of us live an ungodly life in its godless system. It is attempting to mold us to its sinful image.

The flesh, or the old nature, wants us to continue to live as we did before we became believers. Instead of godly desires, the old nature promotes selfish desires.

The devil is a real person—a being who wants believers to fail. He, through his emissaries, attempts to cause us to fail.

It is important that we have an understanding of these three enemies and how they are trying to cause us to sin.

2. REALIZE THAT CHRIST HAS WON THE VICTORY

Second, understand that Jesus Christ has won the victory over these enemies. Paul wrote about the ability we have to demolish these spiritual strongholds. He put it this way:

> For the weapons of our warfare are not human weapons, but are made powerful by God for tearing down strongholds. We tear down arguments and every arrogant obstacle that is raised up against the knowledge of God, and we take every thought captive to make it obey Christ (2 Corinthians 10:4,5 NET).

We possess spiritual weapons, provided by Jesus Christ, with which to fight the spiritual battle. We need to take hold of these weapons and use them as they are meant to be used. When we use these weapons, as they were designed, we can then win the spiritual battles we face.

Indeed, the Bible says that the devil has been rendered powerless. The writer to the Hebrews emphasized that Jesus has defeated the devil:

> Since the children have flesh and blood, he too shared in their humanity so that by his death he might break the power of him who holds the power of death—that is, the devil (Hebrews 2:14 NIV).

He is powerless to defeat us.

John said that the coming of Jesus was to destroy the works of the devil. He wrote:

> He who sins is of the devil, for the devil has sinned from the beginning. For this purpose the Son of God was manifested, that He might destroy the works of the devil (1 John 3:8 NKJV).

Therefore, the victory has been won—we do not have to keep on sinning. This is a message the devil does not want us to hear.

3. WE HAVE TO WANT TO GET RID OF THE SIN

Next, we have to want this habitual sin to be overcome. This is crucial. Without the desire on our part, the habitual sin that plagues us will continue to be a source of defeat.

In His model prayer for His disciples, Jesus illustrated how we should pray in a situation like this. He said:

> And do not lead us into temptation, but deliver us from the evil one (Matthew 6:13 NET).

As much as we are able, we should not place ourselves in any situation where we could fall into sin. This may include taking some specific steps on our part. Whatever we need to do, we must do it so that we won't be caught up in habitual sin.

4. THE VICTORY MUST BE ACCEPTED BY FAITH

Finally, by faith, we have to receive the victory that Christ has given us. We are to walk in faith, believing the promises of Christ. For example, Satan will flee from us if we resist him. James stated it in this manner:

> So submit to God. But resist the devil and he will flee from you (James 4:7 NET).

If we submit to God, the victory can be ours.

The good news is that we do not have to sin. We can only blame ourselves when we sin. God has promised to provide a way out. We must accept by faith the provisions that God has made for us.

SUMMARY TO QUESTION 35
HOW CAN WE OVERCOME HABITUAL SIN?

According to the Bible, no believer has to be in habitual sin. If anyone is troubled by one or two sinful habits that they cannot break, there are certain promises in Scripture that will help us overcome these habits.

First, we must realize who our enemies are—the world, the flesh, and the devil. The world system tries to mold us into its ungodly ways. The flesh, or old nature, tries to have us act selfishly. The devil, a personal being, does everything he can to keep us from following Christ. We must understand how they are trying to cause us to sin.

Once we realize who these enemies are, we then must realize that these enemies hold no power over us—Jesus Christ has defeated them. Because we belong to Jesus, we too can defeat them. He has provided us with the spiritual weapons necessary for victory.

We must then realize that God has provided a way out from our sin. There is a way of escape from our dilemma.

However, we must want to get rid of the sin. We cannot achieve victory without a desire to do so.

We must accept the victory by faith. This includes submitting these particular sins to God, and then fleeing from any situation that may arise.

If we do this, then we can overcome habitual sin.

What Is the Forgiveness of Sins?

The word "forgiveness" is one of the key terms in the vocabulary of Scripture. It is very important that we have an understanding of exactly what it is.

FORGIVENESS DEFINED

Forgiveness can be defined as "the act of not holding someone's sin against them." When someone intentionally wrongs, or injures us, we are not to hold this against them—we are to forgive their actions.

When people sin against God, *only* God can forgive them. We do not have the authority to forgive anyone who sins against God.

There are a number of important points about how God, through Jesus Christ, forgives sins. They include the following:

1. CHRISTIAN FORGIVENESS IS BASED UPON THE DEATH OF JESUS CHRIST

The Bible says that Jesus Christ has forgiven all those who come to Him in faith. This forgiveness is based upon His death on Calvary's cross. On the night of His betrayal, Jesus told His disciples the following:

> For this is my blood, which seals the covenant between God
> and his people. It is poured out to forgive the sins of many
> (Matthew 26:28 NLT).

Jesus' blood, or His death, is the basis on which human beings can be forgiven. Indeed, it is the only basis.

The Apostle Paul also stated that Christians are now forgiven of their sins in the sight of God. He wrote the following to the Colossians:

> When you were dead in your sins and in the uncircumcision
> of your flesh, God made you alive with Christ. He forgave us
> all our sins (Colossians 2:13 NIV).

Formerly, we were dead in our sins, but now, because of what Jesus has done on our behalf, we have been forgiven.

The Apostle John emphasized that our sins have been forgiven because of Jesus' name, or authority. He put it like this:

> I am writing to you, little children, that your sins have been
> forgiven because of his name (1 John 2:12 NET).

It is Jesus' death that is the basis of Christian forgiveness. This is one of the key truths of the New Testament.

2. HIS BLOOD HAD TO BE SHED

The writer to the Hebrews emphasized the biblical principle that there could be no forgiveness unless blood was shed. He wrote the following:

> Indeed, under the law almost everything is purified with
> blood, and without the shedding of blood there is no for-
> giveness of sins (Hebrews 9:22 NKJV).

Without the shedding of blood, or death, forgiveness is not possible.

Paul also emphasized that the forgiveness of sin was linked to the blood, or the death, of Christ. He said to the Ephesians:

> In him we have redemption through his blood, the forgiveness of our trespasses, according to the riches of his grace (Ephesians 1:7 NET).

Therefore, divine forgiveness—the forgiveness between God and the sinner—is based upon the death of Jesus Christ upon the cross of Calvary. Those who have come to Him in faith will have their sins forgiven. This is what the Scripture promises.

3. THERE IS A DIFFERENCE BETWEEN HUMAN AND DIVINE FORGIVENESS

There is a huge difference between human and divine forgiveness. Human beings can only forgive sin that has been committed personally against them. Indeed, we cannot forgive someone for committing a sin against someone else. We can only forgive someone who has sinned against us.

Divine forgiveness extends to everyone who has sinned against God. This includes all of us. Therefore, since all of us have sinned against God, it is possible that all of us can be forgiven of our sins.

We read in the Book of Acts:

> All the prophets testify about him that everyone who believes in him receives forgiveness of sins through his name (Acts 10:43 NIV).

Everyone who believes in Christ can receive His forgiveness. The divine forgiveness is available to all of humanity.

4. FORGIVENESS IS THROUGH JESUS CHRIST ALONE

It is through the Person of Jesus Christ, and Him alone, that this forgiveness of sin occurs. John wrote the following:

My little children, these things I write to you, so that you may not sin. And if anyone sins, we have an Advocate with the Father, Jesus Christ the righteous. And He Himself is the propitiation for our sins, and not for ours only but also for the whole world (1 John 2:1,2 NKJV).

There is no one else who can forgive our sins. Only Jesus can do this. This is the consistent testimony of the Bible.

This sums up some of the key points which the Scripture makes concerning forgiveness of sins. It is vital that we understand these important things.

SUMMARY TO QUESTION 36
WHAT IS THE FORGIVENESS OF SINS?

Forgiveness of sin is an extremely important topic. Forgiveness can be defined as the act of not holding sin against someone.

For the human race, forgiveness of sin is based upon the death of Jesus Christ on the cross of Calvary. Scripture emphasizes that the blood He shed upon the cross is the only basis of God's divine forgiveness.

We must also appreciate that there is a huge difference between human forgiveness and divine forgiveness. Humans can only forgive sin that is personally committed against them. We have no authority to forgive people who have sinned against others, or who have sinned against God.

However, everyone has sinned against God. Indeed, the entire human race is born separated from God because of sin. Therefore, it is possible for God to forgive anyone who confesses his or her sin.

Finally, Scripture makes it clear that it is through Jesus Christ, and Him alone, that a person can be forgiven of their sins. Forgiveness from God, apart from Christ, is not possible.

What Role Does Jesus Play with the Father Concerning Our Forgiveness? (Advocacy)

When it comes to the forgiveness of our sins, Jesus Christ occupies the central role. In fact, Scripture speaks of believers having an "advocate" with the Father. The Apostle John wrote the following about the present work of Jesus:

> My dear children, I write this to you so that you will not sin. But if anybody does sin, we have an advocate with the Father—Jesus Christ, the Righteous One. He is the atoning sacrifice for our sins, and not only for ours but also for the sins of the whole world (1 John 2:1,2 NIV).

The New Living Translation puts it this way:

> My dear children, I am writing this to you so that you will not sin. But if you do sin, there is someone to plead for you before the Father. He is Jesus Christ, the one who pleases God completely. He is the sacrifice for our sins. He takes away not only our sins but the sins of all the world (1 John 2:1,2 NLT).

An advocate is one who speaks in a person's defense. Advocacy, therefore, is the work of Christ on behalf of believers that sin.

THIS IS NOT THE SAME AS FORGIVENESS OF SIN AT THE TIME OF SALVATION

This is not the same thing as forgiveness of sins for eternal salvation. That occurs once and for all when a person becomes a believer in Christ. At that time, all of their sins have been forgiven—past, present, and future. There is no more judgment, or condemnation, for those who believe in Christ. Their sins have been removed. The psalmist described the situation in this manner:

> As far as the eastern horizon is from the west, so he removes the guilt of our rebellious actions from us (Psalm 103:12 NET).

Our sins have been removed as far as the east is from the west. In other words, forgiveness is complete.

In the Book of Micah, it is illustrated in this way:

> You will again have compassion on us; you will tread our sins underfoot and hurl all our iniquities into the depths of the sea. (Micah 7:19 NIV).

Our sins are buried at the bottom of the sea. In other words, they are gone forever.

Therefore, the believer does not have to eternally answer to God for his or her sins. They have been totally forgiven.

CHRISTIANS STILL COMMIT SIN

However, a believer still sins. Therefore, something has to be done with the daily sins that we commit. This is why we need the ministry of Jesus Christ's advocacy. As advocate, He represents us to God the Father

Once the sin question has been dealt with, it is now up to the believer to experience their daily cleaning from the defilements of sin.

The psalmist testified:

> He restores my strength (Psalm 23:3 NET).

This is the job of the Lord Jesus—it is the restoration of our strength.

Paul wrote about the cleansing that Jesus Christ gave to those who believed. He wrote the following to the Church at Ephesus:

> Husbands, love your wives just as Christ loved the church and gave himself for her to sanctify her by cleansing her with the washing of the water by the word, so that he may present the church to himself as glorious—not having a stain or wrinkle, or any such blemish, but holy and blameless (Ephesians 5:25-27 NET).

Our sins have been taken away by Christ. John wrote:

> This is He who came by water and blood—Jesus Christ; not only by water, but by water and blood. And it is the Spirit who bears witness, because the Spirit is truth (1 John 5:6 NKJV).

Therefore, we confess our sins to Jesus Christ, our Advocate.

JESUS DEFENDS US FROM ACCUSATIONS

He also defends us from accusations made against us. Satan constantly makes accusations against believers before God. We read in the Book of Revelation:

> Then I heard a loud voice in heaven say: "Now have come the salvation and the power and the kingdom of our God, and the authority of his Messiah. For the accuser of our brothers and sisters, who accuses them before our God day and night, has been hurled down (Revelation 12:10 NIV).

It is Jesus Christ who is constantly defending the believer. Since we are still in these sinful bodies, we certainly need His defense!

This sums up the important role of Jesus Christ, our Advocate.

SUMMARY TO QUESTION 15
WHAT ROLE DOES JESUS PLAY WITH THE FATHER CONCERNING OUR FORGIVENESS? (ADVOCACY)

One of the present ministries of Jesus is that of "advocacy." Scripture says that Jesus Christ is our Advocate with God the Father. He is the One who pleads our case before God the Father so that we can experience forgiveness of sin. Yet, this forgiveness is not for our eternal salvation. That has already occurred in the past. This advocacy is for Christians who sin after they have believed. When we sin, we need someone to plead our case with God the Father. This is what Jesus does for us today.

This advocacy is necessary because of the constant accusations against us by the devil. Jesus, thus, is constantly defending us.

Whom Are Believers
Supposed to Forgive?

God has forgiven believers for every sin they have committed: past, present, and future. This is the good news, the gospel! This being the case, who then, are believers supposed to forgive? What does the Scripture say?

1. WE ARE TO FORGIVE EVERYONE

The Bible is very clear on this matter. It says we are supposed to forgive everyone—there are no exceptions to this. Paul made this clear as he wrote the following to the Ephesians. He stated it this way:

> Get rid of all bitterness, rage and anger, brawling and slander, along with every form of malice. Be kind and compassionate to one another, forgiving each other, just as in Christ God forgave you (Ephesians 4:31,32 NIV).

Forgiveness should extend to everyone.

2. FORGIVENESS MUST BE COMPLETE

Forgiveness should not only extend to every human being, forgiveness should also be complete—we are not to hold anything against anyone. No matter what a person has done to us, we need to forgive them.

3. WE ARE TO FORGIVE WHENEVER WE ARE ASKED

There is one other thing. Jesus taught that we are supposed to forgive people as often as they ask for it. Luke records Him saying:

> Even if he wrongs you seven times a day and each time turns again and asks forgiveness, forgive him (Luke 17:4 NLT).

In other words, every time someone sins against us and asks for forgiveness we are to, in turn, forgive them.

In another place, we read of Jesus emphasizing this same truth:

> Then Peter came to Jesus and asked, "Lord, how many times shall I forgive my brother or sister who sins against me? Up to seven times?" Jesus answered, "I tell you, not seven times, but seventy-seven times (Matthew 18:21,22 NIV).

Therefore, the New Testament idea for forgiveness is simple: believers are to forgive everyone who has sinned against them, and we are to forgive everything which they have done to us.

In addition, we are to forgive them as many times as they ask. Forgiveness, therefore, is to be to everyone, and it is to be complete. This is the biblical way.

SUMMARY TO QUESTION 38
WHOM ARE BELIEVERS SUPPOSED TO FORGIVE?

Believers in Jesus Christ are supposed to forgive others. The Lord commands us to do so. There are a number of aspects to this forgiveness and, it is important that we understand what He teaches about them.

First, the Bible says that we are to forgive everyone. There are no exceptions to this. No matter what someone may do to us, if they ask our forgiveness, then we are required to forgive them. This is based upon what Jesus has done for us. Because He has forgiven us of all of our sins, we are to forgive everyone who sins against us.

Furthermore, the forgiveness is to be complete. This means that whatever they have done to us should be forgiven—we don't hold anything back. Every wrong they have committed against us must be forgiven.

Thirdly, as many times as they ask our forgiveness, we are to forgive them. In other words, our forgiveness is to be unlimited.

This illustrates the type of forgiveness which the Lord has extended to us. Our sins, though many, have been forgiven, and forgotten. This is true of any sins which we may commit in the future. In the same manner, we are to forgive others. In doing so, we honor the Lord and His Word.

How Do We Treat Someone Who Sins Against Us?

When someone sins against us, what should we do? How should we react? What does the Lord expect from us?

In Matthew's gospel, Jesus tells us how to confront sin that has been carried out against us. He said the following:

> If your brother sins, go and show him his fault when the two of you are alone. If he listens to you, you have regained your brother. But if he does not listen, take one or two others with you, that *at the testimony of two or three witnesses every matter may be established*. If he refuses to listen to them, tell it to the church. If he refuses to listen to the church, treat him like a Gentile or tax collector (Matthew 18:15-17 NET).

JESUS TELLS US WHAT TO DO

From these words of Jesus, we can outline the following steps in dealing with someone who has wronged us.

1. WE SHOULD FIRST GO TO THE PERSON

The first thing we are to do is to go that person directly, and attempt to settle it between the two of us. If this can be done, then the matter is closed, and nothing further should be said. This should always be the first step.

2. NEXT, WE SHOULD TAKE ALONG OTHERS

If the person will not listen to us, then we take along others; and, again, confront that person—this time in front of witnesses. If the person repents, then the matter is settled.

3. FINALLY, WE TAKE THEM BEFORE THE CHURCH

If the person refuses to do anything about it, we then take them before the church. The issue needs to be discussed before the believers. If they still refuse to repent, they are to be considered as an outcast until they have a change of heart.

If that person repents, then they are to be restored to the congregation. Restoration consists of confession, and then repentance.

4. CONFESSION MUST BE MADE BEFORE RESTORATION

To be restored, the person must first confess their sin. This means they must admit that it is sin, and not try to whitewash it, or blame it on someone else. In other words, they must take complete responsibility for what they have done.

5. THERE MUST BE TRUE REPENTANCE

Furthermore, the person must repent asking God to forgive them, and then to help them from continuing to commit the sin. The Bible says the following:

> If we confess our sins, he is faithful and just to forgive us our sins and to cleanse us from all unrighteousness (1 John 1:9 ESV).

There must be a true repentance.

6. IF A PERSON CONFESSES AND REPENTS, THEY SHOULD BE RESTORED

If the person confesses their sin, and repents of what they have done, they are then restored to fellowship. In God's eyes, the sin has been forgiven, and it should never again be brought to one's attention.

The psalmist wrote:

> As far as the east is from the west, so far has he removed our transgressions from us (Psalm 103:12 NIV).

Therefore, we should not only forgive the person, we should not hold it against them. It is time to move on. This is what the Bible commands.

SUMMARY TO QUESTION 39
HOW DO WE TREAT SOMEONE WHO SINS AGAINST US?

There are a number of steps to take when someone sins against us. If that person does not repent, the Bible provides a process that should be followed.

This includes first going to the person. Hopefully the matter can be settled that way.

If the person still does not repent, then we take someone with us. This is the next step.

If they still refuse to listen, we then take them before the church. The believers, the body of Christ, need to hear the matter.

However, if they still refuse to listen, then they should be considered an outcast until there is genuine repentance.

If a person confesses their sin and repents, then that person should be restored. Restoration is always the final goal.

Once restored, the sin should be put in the past, and should not be held against that person.

QUESTION 40

What If We Do Not Feel Like Forgiving Someone Who Has Hurt Us?

All human beings, sooner or later, will be hurt by other people. On many occasions, the hurt is deeply painful.

Truth be told, there are times when we, as Christians, simply do not feel like forgiving someone who has hurt us—although we know that this is what we are supposed to do.

What do we do? What are some of the practical steps which we can take in these types of situations?

BELIEVERS MUST REALIZE THAT WE ARE REQUIRED TO FORGIVE

To begin with, we must realize that the Bible requires those who believe in Jesus Christ to forgive everyone who has sinned against them. There are no exceptions.

Indeed, Jesus made it clear that we are to forgive others in the same way as He has forgiven us. Matthew records Him saying the following:

> But if you refuse to forgive others, your Father will not forgive your sins (Matthew 6:15 NLT).

As believers in Jesus Christ, we have no choice—we must forgive the person who does us wrong.

Paul wrote to the Ephesians about this need to forgive:

> Be kind and compassionate to one another, forgiving each other, just as in Christ God forgave you (Ephesians 4:32 NIV)

We must forgive like He has forgiven us. In other words, there must be complete forgiveness. This first point is non-negotiable.

WE FORGIVE NO MATTER HOW MANY TIMES THEY WRONG US

This second point follows the first. Not only are we required to forgive those who have hurt us, we are commanded to forgive the offender as often as they sin against us. Jesus made this very clear:

> Peter came up to the Lord and asked, "How many times should I forgive someone who does something wrong to me? Is seven times enough?" Jesus answered: Not just seven times, but seventy-seven times! (Matthew 18:21 CEV).

According to the Lord, every time someone asks us for forgiveness, we are to forgive them. Again, no exceptions.

3. WE ARE TO NOT SEEK VENGEANCE AGAINST THE PERSON

This brings us to our next point. We are not only commanded to forgive the offender, as well as forgive them as many times as they ask for forgiveness, we are also not to seek vengeance against them.

The Bible is very clear on this point! We allow the Lord to take His vengeance upon the person. This is not our responsibility.

In fact, Paul wrote the following to the Romans about the believer and the idea of vengeance:

Beloved, never avenge yourselves, but leave it to the wrath of God, for it is written, "Vengeance is mine, I will repay, says the Lord" (Romans 12:19 ESV).

It is not for believers in Christ to seek vengeance. The Lord will take care of any vengeance, if necessary. We must let Him do His work. He will, in His time.

Humanly speaking, this is very difficult, if not impossible, to do. Consequently, we should admit to the Lord, in prayer, that we need help with this matter. He has promised to answer this type of prayer:

Pray to me in time of trouble. I will rescue you, and you will honor me (Psalm 50:15 CEV).

He will deliver us from our desire for vengeance—if we call upon Him to do so. This is His promise to us.

4. WE SHOULD PRAY FOR THE PERSON WHO HAS SINNED AGAINST US

How can we not want to avenge ourselves against someone who has wronged us? In many cases, this seems difficult, if not impossible. This next point should be helpful in answering this question.

If we have a difficult time in forgiving someone, one of the ways which can be helpful is that we pray for that person. Indeed, it is very hard to stay angry at a person that you are praying for.

In fact, this is exactly what Jesus told us to do:

But I tell you to love your enemies and pray for anyone who mistreats you (Matthew 5:44 CEV).

Consequently, if we truly want to forgive someone who has wronged us, then we will pray for that person.

Again, humanly speaking, this is not an easy thing to do. Nevertheless, we must do it.

WHAT SHOULD WE ASK THE LORD TO DO FOR THEM?

In obedience to the commands of the Lord, we should want the best for our enemies. Asking the Lord in prayer to cause that person to follow Christ, and to walk the straight and narrow, will go a long way toward helping us obey what He commands about forgiveness. This, of course, is not something we can do in our own strength.

5. WE SHOULD SEE THE PERSON AS GOD SEES THEM

Another practical step toward forgiving someone from our heart, concerns the way the Lord views the person. When we pray, we should ask the Lord to reveal to us how He sees this individual. In other words, what does the offending person look like before the Lord? What is God's perspective on the matter?

Jesus saw the multitudes as lost and confused:

> But when He saw the multitudes, He was moved with compassion for them, because they were weary and scattered, like sheep having no shepherd (Matthew 9:36 NKJV).

It is highly possible, if not likely, that the Lord sees this offending person in the same way. If this is the case, then we should view this person in the same way as Christ does—a human being who desperately needs the direction of the Lord.

Consequently, if we see them as Jesus sees them, we will want God's best for them—not the worst.

As we continue to emphasize, humanly speaking, this is very difficult to do. This is why we need the leading of the Holy Spirit when we truly forgive people.

6. WE MUST APPRECIATE THAT FORGIVENESS WILL TAKE TIME

Another crucial point to remember is that forgiveness takes time—it doesn't usually happen immediately. While God forgives instantly those who confess their sin, it is not always the same for us.

This is especially true if this person has done terrible, hurtful things, either to us, or to those whom we love. Consequently, it is difficult to forgive that individual right away.

Again, this is where we need the supernatural work of the Holy Spirit. He allows us to forgive people when otherwise we would not be willing to forgive.

7. WE WILL NEVER COMPLETELY FORGET WHAT THE PERSON DID

The Bible says that the God of the Bible does not hold the sin against the person who has sinned against Him. The Lord has said:

> I—yes, I alone—am the one who blots out your sins for my own sake and will never think of them again (Isaiah 43:25 NLT).

When it says that He will never think of them again, this does not mean He forgets that they ever happened in the sense that He does not remember the episode.

On the contrary, it means He does not hold the sin against the person. As far as Christ is concerned, that event never happened.

As humans, we are certainly not able to forget what an offending person has done to us in the sense that we cannot remember it any longer. However, like God, we should not hold the sin against the person.

Paul wrote to the Philippians:

> My friends, I don't feel that I have already arrived. But I forget what is behind, and I struggle for what is ahead (Philippians 3:13 CEV).

We must put the past behind us, the best that we can, and then move ahead.

DO NOT BECOME OBSESSED BY IT!

While we cannot totally forget what people have done to us, we do not have to be obsessed by it. We must refuse to let it control the way in which we live.

Unfortunately, too many people hold on to bitterness against someone for something they have done to hurt either them, or a loved one. For whatever reason, they cannot, or will not, let go of it.

Above all, we should not let this sort of bitterness get hold of us. We are warned about this in Scripture:

> See to it that no one fails to obtain the grace of God; that no "root of bitterness" springs up and causes trouble, and by it many become defiled (Hebrews 12:15 ESV).

With God's grace, we need to move on. If we do not, we are the only ones who will be hurt.

8. FORGIVENESS DOES NOT MEAN THAT WE HAVE TO RECONCILE

This next point cannot be emphasized enough: Forgiveness is not reconciliation!

While the best thing that could possibly happen is that we can reconcile with the person who has harmed us, truth be told, in many instances, this is not possible, or even realistic.

However, many believers make the mistake of thinking that if they forgive someone who has offended them, then they must reconcile with them.

There are two people involved—the one forgiving and the one forgiven. There are instances when the one forgiven will not want to be reconciled with us.

Indeed, they may feel they have nothing in which to be forgiven! For whatever reason, they may believe that they have done absolutely nothing wrong.

Since they assume their behavior has not been sinful, they insist that there is nothing to forgive. It is clear that we cannot do anything about this type of response.

However, we are responsible for the way we respond in these situations. Obviously, it can get very complicated and reconciling is sometimes nearly impossible.

WE NEED TO PROTECT OURSELVES

There is something else. It is also possible that the one who has harmed us is likely to do it again, if given another chance. This is where we must use wisdom. The fact that we have forgiven someone does not necessarily mean that we have to place ourselves in a similar situation with that person. Forgiving someone does not mean that we have to act unwisely toward them.

Therefore, we must ask the Lord for wisdom when it comes to dealing with someone whom we have forgiven.

LET US REMEMBER WHAT THE LORD HAS FORGIVEN US FOR

This last point should put the entire issue of forgiveness into proper perspective. As Christians, we have experienced the forgiveness of God for all of our sins. The fact that God has forgiven us for everything that we have ever said, or have ever done, should make it easier for us to forgive someone for a particular wrong. Jesus illustrated this in one of His parables:

> Therefore the kingdom of heaven may be compared to a king who wished to settle accounts with his servants. When he began to settle, one was brought to him who owed him ten thousand talents. And since he could not pay, his master ordered him to be sold, with his wife and children and all that he had, and payment to be made. So the servant fell on his knees, imploring him, 'Have patience with me, and I

will pay you everything.' And out of pity for him, the master of that servant released him and forgave him the debt. But when that same servant went out, he found one of his fellow servants who owed him a hundred denarii, and seizing him, he began to choke him, saying, 'Pay what you owe.' So his fellow servant fell down and pleaded with him, 'Have patience with me, and I will pay you.' He refused and went and put him in prison until he should pay the debt. When his fellow servants saw what had taken place, they were greatly distressed, and they went and reported to their master all that had taken place. Then his master summoned him and said to him, 'You wicked servant! I forgave you all that debt because you pleaded with me. And should not you have had mercy on your fellow servant, as I had mercy on you?' And in anger his master delivered him to the jailers, until he should pay all his debt. So also my heavenly Father will do to every one of you, if you do not forgive your brother from your heart (Matthew 18:22-35 ESV).

The truth of this story should be at the basis of our view of our forgiveness of others. Since God has forgiven us for everything that we have ever done, it is not too much to ask of us to forgive another person for what they have done to us.

REMEMBER WHAT CHRIST HAS DONE FOR US

So, we need to remind ourselves what Christ has done for us. Three things should be mentioned.

HE HAS FORGIVEN EVERY SIN THAT WE HAVE COMMITTED

The Bible says that our sins have been forgiven as far as the East is from the West:

How far has the Lord taken our sins from us? Farther than the distance from east to west! (Psalm 103:12 CEV)

Scripture also says that they have been buried in the bottom of the ocean:

> Our God, no one is like you. We are all that is left of your chosen people, and you freely forgive our sin and guilt. You don't stay angry forever; You're glad to have pity and pleased to be merciful. You will trample on our sins and throw them in the sea (Micah 7:18,19 CEV).

We should never forget this!

HE HAS GIVEN US ETERNAL LIFE

Forgiven sinners are also given eternal life by our gracious God:

> For God so loved the world, that he gave his only Son, that whoever believes in him should not perish but have eternal life (John 3:16 ESV).

HE HAS MADE US CO-HEIRS WITH HIM

Finally, we have not only been forgiven and given eternal life, but we have also been made co-heirs with Him.

> The Spirit himself bears witness with our spirit that we are children of God, and if children, then heirs—heirs of God and fellow heirs with Christ, provided we suffer with him in order that we may also be glorified with him (Romans 8:16,17 ESV).

Many of the things that belong to Him now belong to us. Since the Lord has done all of this for us, it is certainly not too much to ask that we forgive others, no matter how bad they have hurt us.

This sums up some of the important things that we should remember if we get to the place where we do not feel like forgiving someone who has hurt us deeply.

SUMMARY TO QUESTION 40
WHAT IF WE DO NOT FEEL LIKE FORGIVING SOMEONE WHO HAS HURT US?

There are many times when we, as believers, do not want to forgive people for what they have done to us. In fact, they may have hurt us so deeply, that we do not ever want to forgive them, even though we know that we should.

There are a number of things that we should remember in times like this.

First, we are commanded by Jesus to forgive, there are no exceptions. Thus, holding back our forgiveness is not an option for Christians.

Second, forgiveness is complete. In other words, we forgive people as often as they ask for forgiveness—we never stop. There is no limit to our forgiving others.

Third, when we forgive others, we must give up any desire on our part to take vengeance upon that person. Any vengeance, if necessary, must be carried out by the Lord, and by Him alone.

Fourth, we should pray for God's best for the person who wronged us. Jesus has commanded us to do this. True forgiveness wishes the best, not the worst, for those who have wronged us. To do this takes a supernatural work from the Lord!

Fifth, it helps if we see that person as God sees them: lost and confused. This can go a long way toward us having a forgiving heart toward them.

Sixth, we must realize that forgiveness takes time. Try as we might, we should not assume that we will be able to forgive them immediately.

Seventh, we cannot entirely forget what the person has done to us. It is not possible for this to happen. However, we must move forward with our life, and not be obsessed with the hurt that the person has caused us.

The eighth point to remember is that forgiveness does not mean reconciling with the person. It would be wonderful if we could be made right with the person; yet, this is not always possible, or realistic. This is especially the case when the other person does not think they have wronged us. Nevertheless, we should try, as much as possible, to make things right with this person we are forgiving. However, forgiveness is not reconciliation!

Finally, it is much easier to forgive a person when we realize the forgiveness that the Lord has extended to us. Indeed, He has forgiven us for every sin which we have committed. When we put the matter into perspective, we understand that the Lord is not really asking that much from us.

These points are essential to realize if we want to forgive others as Christ has commanded. However, we are not claiming that it will be easy, but it is the right thing to do.

How Does God Work
With Our Conscience?

It is important to understand the place our conscience has in our Christian experience. Indeed, it is a central part of our overall makeup. There are a number of things that the Bible says about the conscience.

WHAT IS THE CONSCIENCE?

Our conscience can be defined as that inner voice inside of each of us that tells us what we should do.

In fact, God spoke to the prophet Elijah through a still small voice that we can identify as his conscience. The Bible says:

God said, "Go out and stand in front of the Lord on the mountain."

> As the Lord was passing by, a fierce wind tore mountains and shattered rocks ahead of the Lord. But the Lord was not in the wind. After the wind came an earthquake. But the Lord wasn't in the earthquake. After the earthquake there was a fire. But the Lord wasn't in the fire. And after the fire there was a quiet, whispering voice (1 Kings 19:11,12 God's Word).

Everyone, believer and unbeliever both, has a conscience. However, the conscience of the Christian is certainly different from that of the non-Christian.

We can make the following observations about what the Bible has to say about the conscience:

OUR CONSCIENCE WAS EVIL BEFORE WE BECAME BELIEVERS IN JESUS

Before a person trusts Christ as Savior, their conscience is described as evil. The writer to the Hebrews said:

> Let us draw near with a true heart in full assurance of faith, having our hearts sprinkled from an evil conscience and our bodies washed with pure water (Hebrews 10:22 NKJV).

This does not mean that all we thought about was evil, rather it means that nothing in our thoughts were pleasing to God.

Paul emphasized the same thing to Titus. He wrote:

> All is pure to those who are pure. But to those who are corrupt and unbelieving, nothing is pure, but both their mind and conscience are corrupted (Titus 1:15 NET).

This is further stressed by what Paul wrote to Timothy. He stated that the conscience of false teachers is dead. He said:

> These teachers are hypocrites and liars. They pretend to be religious, but their consciences are dead (1 Timothy 4:2 NLT).

Therefore, the conscience of the unbeliever cannot think thoughts that God is pleased with. It is something beyond its capability.

THE CONSCIENCE OF THE BELIEVER IS DIFFERENT

However, the believer has a conscience which has been redeemed, it is no longer dead. Indeed, we can now think God's thoughts.

WHAT THE BELIEVER IS TO DO WITH THEIR CONSCIENCE

Since believers have a conscience that is redeemed, and can think God's thoughts, what should we do with our conscience? The Bible tells us that there are a number of things that we should do. This includes the following:

WE ARE NOT TO DO ANYTHING AGAINST OUR CONSCIENCE

To begin with, the Bible says we should not violate, or do anything that is against our conscience. Paul wrote to the Romans:

> But if a person has doubts and still eats, he is condemned because he didn't act in faith. Anything that is not done in faith is sin (Romans 14:23 God's Word).

Our conscience has been given to us to guide us. It should not be ignored.

The Apostle Paul gave examples of people who violated their conscience. Indeed, he specifically named two individuals who were guilty of this:

> Cling tightly to your faith in Christ, and always keep your conscience clear. For some people have deliberately violated their consciences; as a result, their faith has been shipwrecked. Hymenaeus and Alexander are two examples of this. I turned them over to Satan so they would learn not to blaspheme God (1 Timothy 1:19,20 NLT).

If we cannot do something in good conscience, then we should simply not do it.

OUR CONSCIENCE SHOULD ALWAYS BE SUBORDINATE TO SCRIPTURE

It must be emphasized that the conscience must always be subordinated to the revealed Word of God. Oftentimes people say that they do not feel convicted of committing something that the Bible clearly says is sin. Because their conscience does not bother them, they feel that they should continue with what they are doing.

However, if God has objectively said that a certain act is wrong, then it is *always* wrong. Lack of any feeling of conviction does not make the deed right.

OUR CONSCIENCE SHOULD BE KEPT CLEAR

We are to keep our conscience clear. Peter wrote about the necessity of doing this. He stated it in this manner:

> Yet do it with courtesy and respect, keeping a good conscience, so that those who slander your good conduct in Christ may be put to shame when they accuse you. For it is better to suffer for doing good, if God wills it, than for doing evil (1 Peter 3:16, 17 NET).

The Apostle Paul testified that he had a good conscience before the Lord.

> Paul looked straight at the Sanhedrin and said, "My brothers, I have fulfilled my duty to God in all good conscience to this day" (Acts 23:1 NIV).

John wrote about believers having a clear conscience. He said:

> Dear friends, if our conscience is clear, we can come to God with bold confidence (1 John 3:21 NLT).

We should pray for a clear conscience. The writer to the Hebrews said:

> Pray for us. Our consciences are clear, and we always try to live right (Hebrews 13:18 CEV).

When our conscience is clear, we can make statements with absolute sincerity and honesty. Paul penned the following to the church at Corinth:

> For our reason for confidence is this: the testimony of our conscience, that with pure motives and sincerity that are from God, not by human wisdom but by the grace of God, we conducted ourselves in the world, and all the more toward you (2 Corinthians 1:12 NET).

Our conscience can also help us in times of persecution. Peter acknowledged this when he wrote to encourage those going through persecution:

> For God is pleased with you when, for the sake of your conscience, you patiently endure unfair treatment (1 Peter 2:19 NLT).

The conscience can be a help to us.

THOSE IN LEADERSHIP SHOULD HAVE A CLEAR CONSCIENCE

Those in leadership must teach others with a clear conscience. Paul wrote to Timothy about the necessary qualifications:

> They must hold the mystery of the faith with a clear conscience (1 Timothy 3:9 ESV).

Paul also said that the purpose of biblical teaching is that all Christians will have a heart that is pure, a conscience that is clear, and a faith in Jesus Christ that is sincere:

> My goal in giving you this order is for love to flow from a pure heart, from a clear conscience, and from a sincere faith (1 Timothy 1:5 God's Word).

Ultimately, the Lord will be the one who examines our conscience.

Paul wrote about this to the Corinthians:

> My conscience is clear, but that isn't what matters. It is the Lord himself who will examine me and decide (1 Corinthians 4:4 NLT).

The Lord Himself is to be the One who examines our conscience.

This sums up some of the essential truths concerning how the Lord works with our conscience. As is readily seen, these truths are necessary to know.

SUMMARY TO QUESTION 41
HOW DOES GOD WORK WITH OUR CONSCIENCE?

The conscience is that inner voice inside each of us. All people have a conscience. This being the case we need to know how the Lord works with it.

Scripture has a number of things to say about the conscience of the believer and the unbeliever.

The Bible says that the conscience of the unbeliever is continually evil. This means there is nothing in their thoughts that are pleasing to God. Nothing.

Better things are said about the conscience of the believer. The Bible encourages believers not to violate their God-given conscience, but rather to make it subordinate to Scripture. The Word of God must be our ultimate guide on what we should do, and what we should not do. Our conscience should not be made the ultimate decision-maker.

Our conscience is there to tell us what is right and what is wrong. This is why God has given it to us.

However, it is possible to ignore what the conscience is saying. This is why it is necessary for it to be under the authority of the Word of God.

About the Author

Don Stewart is a graduate of Biola University and Talbot Theological Seminary (with the highest honors).

Don is a best-selling and award-winning author having authored, or co-authored, over seventy books. This includes the best-selling *Answers to Tough Questions*, with Josh McDowell, as well as the award-winning book *Family Handbook of Christian Knowledge: The Bible*. His various writings have been translated into over thirty different languages and have sold over a million copies.

Don has traveled around the world proclaiming and defending the historic Christian faith. He has also taught both Hebrew and Greek at the undergraduate level and Greek at the graduate level.

Books Available by Don Stewart

The following books are now available from Don Stewart in print as well as in digital format. You can find them at our website www.educatingourworld.com, as well as Amazon and iTunes.

The Bible Series

What Everyone Needs to Know about the Bible
10 Reasons to Trust the Bible

The God Series

Does the God of the Bible Exist?
What Everyone Needs to Know About God
God Has Spoken to Us: Are We Listening?
The Trinity

The Jesus Series

The Case for Christianity
Did Jesus Exist? Are the Records about Him Reliable?
What Everyone Needs to Know about Jesus
The Life and Ministry of Jesus Christ

The Holy Spirit Series

What Everyone Needs to Know About the Holy Spirit
How the Holy Spirit Works in Our Lives
Spiritual Gifts: Part 1: What Are Spiritual Gifts? Are all Spiritual Gifts for Today?
Spiritual Gifts: Part 2: What Are the Various Gifts of the Holy Spirit?
Spiritual Gifts: Part 3: Speaking in Tongues
Divine Healing: Does God Heal Everyone?

The Afterlife Series

Living in the Light of Eternity
What Happens One Second After We Die?
Resurrection and Judgment
Heaven
Hell

The Unseen World Series

Angels
Evil Angels, Demons, and the Occult
Satan

The Last Days Series

The Rapture
The Jews, Jerusalem, and the Coming Temple
In Search of the Lost Ark: The Quest for the Ark of the Covenant
25 Signs We are Near the End

With many more books to come, please check back at our website to discover the latest books we have available.

89990738R00148

Made in the USA
San Bernardino, CA
04 October 2018